KU-013-343

Contents

Acknowledgements

Those of us who write military history know how appreciable they are of any help that they may receive whilst researching and then putting the book together. It is through their commendable efforts that this book was conceived. I acknowledge with grateful thanks, Marcin Zboiska from Poland, who sifted through many hundreds of unpublished images for me. The photographs he found were astounding and have great value and interest to the historian and enthusiast alike.

My debt also goes to Richard White from the USA, who is a serious German photographic album collector. Over the years I have obtained rare original German photographic albums from him and marvelled at the quality of the images inside. My gratitude to Arnim Gerstenmeier from Germany, whose father was an officer in the Wehrmacht, helped me considerably with his own families' personal photographs and letters. The majority of the photographs were taken by Arnim's father and show a multitude of armoured units through the war years on various fronts.

The names of those people I acknowledge have helped me tirelessly with my photographic projects, but there are some contributions to which I must offer a more personal expression of gratitude. My photographic collector and friend Rolf Halfen from Dusseldorf has supplied me with invaluable advice and helped immensely on this project. He has kept in contact with me almost on a day-to-day basis and been patient with my growing demands for rare Panzer images. The majority of the photographs for this book were obtained by Rolf and handed over to me for production. Eighty of the late variant tanks, which appear in this publication, are very rare photographs and were part of a complete photographic album titled, *Panzer Kampf* (Panzer Struggle) 1943-1945. He also found many other rare photographs of Panzer divisions in Yugoslavia and Greece, not to mention dozens of images from the Eastern Front. Anyone that appreciates how difficult it is to obtain good unpublished Panzer photographs, especially late variant models, will undoubtedly understand the effort that has gone into producing this book.

Finally, my appreciation and thanks go to my illustrator and friend Rachael Hudson for her artwork. Rachael is a very talented illustrator. She has always been courteous, helpful and efficient, and has produced outstanding work for me on various projects.

All other images in this book are credited to the HITM Archive. Their website is: www.militaria-net.co.uk/hitm.htm

Panzer Division insignia is by Rachael Hudson of R. Hudson Illustrations.

Foreword

There are many publications that contain lots of interesting photographs of the German Army at war, especially during the Second World War. The majority of the images that have already been published have been obtained from a handful of photographic archives or museums. Frequently these photographs have been used. Although the content matter is generally not disappointing, most of them however are press agency photographs that had been widely used in publications during the war. The majority of them have been seen in newspapers or utilised for German propaganda purposes. Some of them were even published in the famous German war magazine Signal. Almost all of the images available to the public, especially those from Germany, have been repeatedly used after the war in various books, journals and on film. Many of these photographs have in time become instantly recognisable and overused.

Panzer Divisions At War, however, is a collection of a truly unique record of rare and unpublished photographs that were not taken by professional cameramen, but an amateur soldier with a camera. Their intended use was purely a catalogue of personal experiences. The film was developed, probably when on leave from the front, or never developed until after the war. The small prints were often placed with small captions in various private photographic albums, recapturing a soldier's memories of his days fighting with his comrades. There the album, probably marked, *Meine Dienst* (My service) would remain with the veteran until one day after his death, where it would be found in a little back street shop selling house clearance goods, or was simply passed on or sold to an enthusiast or private collector.

The images in this book are not printed from original negatives, but they are good digital replicas scanned to the highest quality from the original print. Although the reader may find the quality of some of the photographs far from perfect, they have not in any way been digitally enhanced or cropped. They are exact copies of the originals and testimony of the amateur photographer who captured a moment of time on the battlefield.

Among the series of photographs is shown the Panzer divisions on the move, resting in various areas of the front, and actually embroiled in combat. Nowhere in the book will the reader find any staged photographs where frontline agency cameramen, working under orders, were unable to take real action shots because of the dangers of battle. What the reader does see is a series of natural uncensored photographs that were taken by the ordinary German soldier during his march with the Panzer divisions.

Combat, as all soldiers know, is an intensely personal, emotional and confusing experience. Events were often misinterpreted, especially by those that actually enacted them. But photographs reflected the visual experiences of the ordinary German soldier, and to a great degree, stimulated distant memories. Each photograph is concerned with individual episodes of historical importance and is a personal exchange between the witness and the reader.

From the early days of training, to the Blitzkrieg campaigns in Poland and France, to the vast expanses of Russia, the deserts of North Africa, and the final battles on the Western and Eastern Fronts, all the photographs in this book depict the story of the Panzer divisions through the photographic lens of the ordinary German soldier. It shows first-hand a vivid record of German armour in action detailing the different elements that went into making up a fully fledged Panzer division; light tanks, main battle tanks, assault guns and anti-tank destroyers, reconnaissance units, support vehicles and of course the Panzergrenadiers or motorised infantry. In-depth descriptive captions also provide much information and facts about the events portrayed. The reader will become aware of the flexibility of the Panzer divisions, which were allowed to dominate military operations for the greater part of World War Two. But throughout the book it is a captured visual account of a part of military history that will hopefully never be forgotten.

Chapter One

Development & Training

The first Panzer training unit saw its debut secretly on 1 November 1933. It was given the code name *Kraftfahrlehrkommando Zossen*. The unit was very limited to the number of machines and was comprised of four *Grosstraktor*, four *Leichttraktor V* and six of the *Kleintraktor* chassis, which had no turrets. The armoured vehicles were clearly not sufficient enough to develop into a tank force. However, by January 1934 driving training commenced, and there was a rapid expansion in the tank forces. By October 1934 the experimental armoured force were distributed within the army. The Panzer division was born.

Although at first the Panzer division was styled as a Cavalry Division, the two were very different. The new Panzer division was composed of two armoured regiments which were supported by a light motorised infantry regiment, an anti-tank battalion, a light artillery regiment, a motorcycle battalion, a signals battalion, and a light combat engineer company. There were even plans at this early stage for a self-propelled artillery battalion. At the outset it was obvious that the Panzer division was an enormous undertaking, which required huge amounts of logistical planning. The first divisions required strength of 13,000 officers and men, which needed some 4,000 vehicles and 481 tracked vehicles to be able to work cohesively and effectively as an armoured force. It was something that could not be undertaken in a short time scale and there were limits to the number of tanks that could be produced. However, Adolf Hitler was in a hurry to develop the Panzer division.

The first tank to be produced in any significant numbers for the new Panzer divisions was the Panzer I or Pz.Kpfw.I, which was known at the time as the MG *Panzerwagen*. Delivery of 318 was made in August 1935, along with 15 of the *Zugfuhrerwagen*, which was later to become the Panzer.III or Pz.Kpfw.III. Throughout this period training and various exercises with these new vehicles continued, with valuable lessons. It soon became apparent that the need for close co-operation between the tanks on the ground and the airforces would be the essential tactical armoured component for a rapid success on the battlefield.

On 15 October 1935 the first three Panzer Divisions were formed. The 1.Panzer-Division, 2.Panzer-Division and the 3.Panzer-Division. The tank component of these first Panzer divisions was to be a Panzer Brigade, initially composed of two tank regiments. The regiments were sub-divided into two battalions or *Abteilungs*. Each *Abteilung* had four companies with 321 light tanks. The complete strength was 561 tanks including command tanks.

In February and March 1936 all three new Panzer divisions took part in extensive training exercises on the proving grounds at Staumuhlen. Although expansion of the Panzer force was still limited in the number of tanks it was allowed to construct, as many as 3,000 Pz.Kpfw. I, II, III tanks had already been produced by the end of 1936. In October 1936 a few of these Panzers actually saw active operations for the first time when a Panzer unit, code named *Abteilung Drohne*, were deployed during the Spanish Civil war to support the Nationalists' drive on Madrid. The tanks were used in numbers for the first time on 11 May 1937 when they took part in a concerted attack on the Spanish Communist positions near Eremita. The Panzer unit remained in Spain for almost two years, and finally returned to Germany in February 1939.

The battlefields of Spain were technically a training exercise for the Panzer and it was soon noted that the light tanks, especially the Pz.Kpfw.I, was an inferior armoured vehicle. In fact, as soon as the Pz.Kpfw.II had become available from October 1936, resources were immediately shifted and there was no effective increase in production of the Pz.Kpfw.I, which remained at about 1350 machines until September 1939.

Tank tacticians like General Heinz Guderian were well aware of the need for more powerful tanks in the new Panzer divisions. The construction of the Pz.Kpfw.III and IV were seen to be the backbone of the new Panzer divisions. These heavier tanks could be used at the most strategically important sectors on the battlefield and employed in mobile operations with the lighter tanks in support. Here they were to widen and exploit breakthroughs created by infantry reserves. The Army High Command envisaged that nine Panzer Divisions should be available by the autumn of 1939. A report made it clear that the men of a Panzer division should consist of the highest fighting spirit and that they were to be considered and developed as an elite unit, especially with regard to their offensive spirit.

Dawn on 13 March 1938 saw the first Panzer division undertake a military operation. The 2.Panzer-Division crossed into Austria. As armoured vehicles, horse drawn transport and infantry poured into Austria, the civilian population greeted them with flowers and ecstatic screams of support. The Panzers too were decorated with greenery and flags from both nations. A multitude of armoured vehicles made their first real appearance, including the Pz.Kpfw.III that had rolled out of production in October 1937. The Pz.Kpfw.IV also made its debut, and only left the assembly lines in January 1938. During its drive across Austria the 2.Panzer-Division covered several hundred miles in forty-eight hours, but lost a third of its tanks due to breakdown. Fortunately the 2.Panzer-Division was not involved in any combat.

Seven months later another Panzer division was once again displaying its might in Europe. This time the 1.Panzer-Division was given the task to capture the Sudetenland. By 10 October 1937 operations were complete. The following year in March 1938 Germany took over the remaining part of Czechoslovakia. Again another single Panzer division was involved in the operation – this time the 3.Panzer-Division. Elements of the division reached Prague within hours of crossing the border. They were followed by the 6.Panzer-Regiment, which rolled in later that same day on 13 March 1939.

Soon after the take over of Czechoslovakia it did not take long before the Panzer force or *Panzerwaffe* incorporated two armoured vehicles that they were currently under Czech manufacture. In due course the 8.Panzer-Division would be equipped with these new Czech tanks – the Pz.Kpfw.35 (t) and the Pz.Kpfw.38 (t), both of which were to see extensive use in Poland.

In the wake of the Czechoslovakian operation the *Panzerwaffe* did not waste time and developed and expanded its armoured force. However, by August 1939 production of armour was clearly not keeping pace with the growing demands of the new Panzer divisions. The strength of the Panzer regiments within the Panzer divisions were therefore revised. Each of the two *Abteilungs* was now composed of two light companies equipped with the Pz.Kpfw.I and II, and one medium company equipped with the Pz.Kpfw.III and IV along with other units. Each *Abteilung* now had 71 to 74 tanks including 5 command tanks, and a regiment now had only 150 to 156 tanks including 12 command tanks. This meant a reduction in strength of a Panzer division from 570 vehicles to some 300. Such a reduction in strength would prove fatal for future operations, especially those Panzer divisions overstretched on the Eastern Front.

An interesting photograph taken in April 1939 showing a group of Pz.Kpfw.I`s and Pz.Kpfw.II`s together with a number of light Horch cross country vehicles and Opel Blitz trucks. The Pz.Kpfw.I was the first light training Panzer built for the *Panzerwaffe* in 1934. Both the Ausf.A and the Ausf.B variants featured a machine-gun armed turret. The vehicle weighed 5.4 tonnes (5.3 tons and was armed with a 7.92mm gun. The Pz.Kpfw.I first saw combat during the Spanish Civil War in 1936 and 1938, but it did not have any real combat potential. Note the white crosses painted on the turrets of the Pz.Kpfw.I`s and Pz.Kpfw.II`s. The crosses were for aerial recognition, but in Poland tank crews soon found that they were easy aiming points for Polish anti-tank gunners. The crosses were later painted over to make them less conspicuous.

Here an Sd.Kfz.251 halftrack during a training exercise. The Sd.Kfz.251 became the most popular German halftrack vehicle during World War Two. These front-wheel steering vehicles with tracked drive transformed the fighting quality of the Panzer divisions. The infantry were trained to ride in these vehicles in order to be carried alongside the advancing Panzers. They brought with them machine-guns, mortars, boxes of ammunition and supplies. The halftrack was also designed to tow anti-tank guns and light anti-aircraft guns, howitzers and pontoon-bridge sections to the forefront of the battle.

A Pz.Kpfw.I with a crew member during a training exercise in 1939. Here in this photograph the 7.92mm machine gun can clearly be seen. Although it was used extensively for training exercises before the war, it was clearly under-gunned and under-armoured and would not be able to fight effectively against heavier and superior enemy tanks. However, this still did not prevent the *Panzerwaffe* from equipping the new Panzer divisions with 1445 of them for war against Poland.

In front of a workshop are two Sd.Kfz.232 *Schwere Panzerspahwägen (6-rad)* parked in a line with a group of motorcycles and a light cross-country vehicle. In this photograph the Sd.Kfz.232 is not yet fitted with the 2cm KwK 30 cannon in its fully traversing turret. During the early part of the war these armoured vehicles were distributed among the Panzer divisions and helped obtain battlefield intelligence.

A group of soldiers pose for the camera whilst wearing their army issue gas masks. They are all inside an Sd.Kfz.251 halftrack during a training exercise. Although the Sd.Kfz.251 was built in relatively small numbers before the war, their success as the preferred vehicle of transport for infantry and reconnaissance units meant that the numbers steadily grew. By 1940 there were 348 produced, and by the end of the war some 16,000 had been built.

A group of motorcyclists together with motorcycle combinations display the versatility of their machines in front of an audience at a training barracks in 1939. The motorcycle was used extensively during the war and a company of them were added to each Panzer division. Their primary role was reconnaissance. The motorcyclists were trained to probe forward, survey enemy positions until they encountered enemy fire and then return with vital information.

During a training exercise in 1939 a Pz.Kpfw.IV rumbles along a dusty road. This vehicle became the most popular of Panzers in the Panzer divisions and remained in production throughout the war. At first it was not intended to be a main armoured vehicle in the *Panzerwaffe*, but it soon proved to be a diverse and effective weapon on the battlefield. The first Pz.Kpfw.IV was produced in 1936. It weighed 17.3 tones (17 tons) and mounted a powerful short-barrelled 7.5cm KwK L/24 gun.

An interesting photograph showing a number of infantry support vehicles of the Lehr-Division in Berlin on 20 April 1939. These vehicles are probably preparing to be paraded along the Unter Linden Strasse in front of Hitler on his birthday. By this period there was a wide variety of infantry support vehicles in Army service. They were a necessity for any Panzer division in maintaining the momentum of an advance, and without support vehicles carrying infantry and other vital supplies, the whole advance might stall.

A group of motorcyclists at a training barracks in 1939. The motorcyclists were trained in many types of combat situations and were taught to ride into battle, dismount and fight, and then quickly retire from enemy contact. In fact, some units that fielded these vehicles were more powerful than the enemy that they would come across.

A motorcycle instructor lectures his new recruits on the art of cross-country driving. On soft ground or bad roads the motorcycle was quite unsuited, despite the machines radically improved performance. It was also vulnerable to small-arms fire and booby traps. But in spite of this, each Panzer division incorporated hundreds of motorcycles, distributed among the Panzer and rifle regiments, flak detachments, artillery regiments, Panzer engineers, supply units, Panzer signals and the reconnaissance units.

Preparing to be moved east, a multitude of various support vehicles belonging to an unidentified Panzer division in 1939. A number of the vehicles can be seen with Pak 35/36 anti-tank guns in tow. A typical Panzer division consisted of literally dozens of different light and heavy support vehicles. Divisional transport amounted to some 900 light and 1100 heavy lorries alone.

At a training barracks in Germany an impressive line of 15cm sFH 18 heavy field howitzers can be seen on tow with a group of halftrack prime movers. Artillery support was crucial for any armoured attack and provided the Panzer divisions with much firepower needed to sustain them in both defensive and offensive roles. It soon became apparent after training that both infantry and motorised artillery regiments were the backbone of the army and paved the way for the Panzer divisions to move forward.

A Pz.Kpfw.I has arrived at a training barracks onboard a specially adapted trailer. The tanks' main armament is temporarily missing. However, eager recruits were still were able to train with the vehicle. The crews that drove them found the Pz.Kpfw.I an excellent training tank and allowed them valuable experience that would carry them through to drive larger and more powerful tanks.

Dressed in the familiar white German training uniform this anti-tank crew pose with a 3.7cm Pak 35/36. This particular gun was used extensively in training and became the standard anti-tank gun used in the Panzer divisions. It weighed only 432kg and had a sloping splinter shield. The gun fired a solid shot round to a maximum range of 4025m.

During an early morning ceremony a commanding officer prepares to decorate a soldier. In the background is a parked Sd.Kfz.231 radio armoured vehicle. This vehicle is armed with a 2cm KwK 30 cannon. It also carries extra radios and a large overhead aerial frame for signals work.

Another military ceremony at a training barracks in 1939. Flanking the commanding officer standing on his podium, are two Pz.Kpfw.38(t)`s. These Czech designed armoured vehicles became the most important tanks used by the *Panzerwaffe* in the early years of the war. It weighed 9.4 tons. Its main armament was a 3.7cm KwK 38 (t) L/47.8 gun and had two 7.92mm MG37 (t) guns for local defence. Approximately 1400 of them entered service and saw extensive action in the Panzer divisions during the early years of the war.

A group of Sd.Kfz.251 halftracks during a parade in 1939. At least 12 to 15 soldiers at a time were able to cram into the small inside area of the vehicle and be carried to the front lines where they would dismount and take up arms against the enemy. Throughout the war the basic vehicle underwent a series of modifications.

A group of Pz.Kpfw.I`s parading inside a stadium surrounded by literally thousands of people. Although this tank was not truly a combat vehicle, it proved to be an excellent training tank. Most of the Panzer crews were trained on the Pz.Kpfw.I until the end of the war or operated it in combat as their first armoured vehicle.

Chapter Two

Blitzkrieg Unleashed – Poland

On 1 September 1939 five German armies unleashed *Fall Weiss* (Case White), the German strategy for the invasion of Poland. Supported by over 3,000 tanks, 10,000 artillery pieces and 1,850,000 infantry attacked Poland using the new Blitzkrieg tactics. In total there were six Panzer Divisions, four Light Divisions and four Motorised Divisions distributed between the 3rd, 4th, 8th, 10th and 14th Armies. In Army Group North General George von Kuechler's 3rd Army attacked from East Prussia with two Infantry Divisions and One Panzer Division. General Gunther von Kluge's 4th Army attacked from Western Pomerania, with eight Infantry Divisions, two Motorised Divisions and one Panzer Division. The strongest complement of the armoured formations, with over 2,000 tanks and 800 armoured cars, in four Panzer Divisions, four Light Divisions and two Motorised Divisions was Colonel General Gerd von Rundstedt's Army Group South, which comprised of the 8th, 10th and 14th Armies.

Units of the *Panzerwaffe* were equipped with 1445 Pz.Kpfw.I's, 1226 Pz.Kpfw.II's, 100 Pz.Kpfw.III's and 211 Pz.Kpfw.IV's. In addition, there were 215 command tanks and other armoured vehicles including the Pz.Kpfw.35(t) and a few Pz.Kpfw.38(t). Along with the tanks, there were some 308 heavy armoured cars and 718 light armoured cars and 68 personnel carriers.

With this overwhelming superiority the Germans used the new Blitzkrieg tactics – highly mobile operations involving the deployment of armour, motorised infantry and airpower in coordinated strikes, thereby achieving rapid penetration followed by the encirclement of an enemy that were totally bound by static and inflexible defensive tactics. Almost immediately the Polish Army found itself reeling back as the strong infantry and Panzer divisions bulldozed their way east towards the Vistula River. Although in some areas the Poles succeeded in stopping the light German tanks, this was quickly neutralised as new Pz.Kpfw.III and Pz.Kpfw.IV medium tanks smashed the enemy positions. The Poles were helpless against these medium German tanks.

The 4.Panzer-Division contained the most medium tanks and was the strongest division in the entire German Army. It was given the most difficult task of driving on Warsaw. By the evening of 8 September, advanced elements arrived on the outskirts of the Polish capital and attempted to storm it. However, the city was well defended and the attack failed with the loss of 57 armoured vehicles.

In spite of the temporary set-back around Warsaw the entire thrust of the Panzer divisions was quick and swift and over the ensuing days both the German Northern and Southern groups continued to make furious thrusts on all fronts. On the Bzura River, remnants of the Poznan and Pomorze armies, now thrown together in a mass of jumbled units made one last desperate attempt and struck out against General Ulex's 10.Panzer-Korps of the 8th Army. What followed was the battle of the Bzura. This was largest infantry and armoured battle of the Polish campaign consisting of nearly 400,000 men.

By 10 September the bulk of the Polish Army had been vanquished. Most of its 30 divisions had been totally destroyed in a vast pincer movement that closed around Warsaw. The pulverising effects of the Blitzkrieg tactics had degenerated the Polish Army into a force that was in a state of panic and confusion. To make matters worse on the 17 September the Russian Army attacked Poland along its former frontier from Latvia in the north down to Romania in the south. In a secret non-aggression pact drawn up in August 1939 Hitler and Stalin had agreed to carve up Poland between themselves. For the Polish armies struggling for survival the situation was now far grimmer. The end had finally come.

By 18 September, besieged by an ever-increasing amount of German infantry, Panzers and aerial support the Polish Army disintegrated, in spite of pockets of strong enemy resistance. The battle of the Bzura alone resulted in the loss of nearly a quarter of the Polish Army. The Panzer divisions had achieved their baptism of fire, and with the support of the infantry and Luftwaffe they had taken just three weeks to defeat the Polish Army. Although the *Panzerwaffe* had dominated the battlefield and completely out-gunned their opponents, losses to armour were still higher than expected. According to German sources 89 Pz.Kpfw.I's, 83 Pz.Kpfw.II's, 26 Pz.Kpfw.III's, 19 Pz.Kpfw.IV's, 7 Pz.Kpfw.35(t)'s, and 7 Pz.Kpfw.38(t)'s were completely written off. In spite of the losses the Germans learned important lessons from the Polish campaign. On the battlefield it was usual for commanders to allot one single Panzer division to spearhead the drives of each army's advance. This had proved ineffective and led to high number of losses. The light divisions were ordered to be slowly withdrawn from Poland and sent back to Germany as the campaign drew to a close. A Panzer regiment was added to each light Panzer division, but by the time it was ready for action the war in Poland was over.

Regardless of the minor setbacks and losses sustained, the Polish campaign demonstrated the speed and power possessed by Panzers and the excellence of the Panzer divisions. The use of the Panzer as an instrument of war ensured the rapid conclusion of the war against Poland. General Heinz Guderian later said that the Panzer divisions played a central role in the Polish campaign. *'Its achievements in these victories'*, he wrote, *'ensured that this new type of strategy would be fundamental to the German campaigns against France and Russia that followed'.*

During the drive through Poland three soldiers pause for a break inside a town and pose for the camera in front of a Pz.Kpfw.III. This vehicle was the *Panzerwaffe*'s first medium Panzer and was the first of six variants produced before July 1940. Note the white crosses painted on the turret and hull. This was very popular, especially during the early phases of the Polish campaign.

On 1 September 1939 the German Army attacked Poland. Here in this photograph is a Pz.Kpfw.II attached to the 1.Panzer-Division during the first few days of the Polish campaign. The Pz.Kpfw.II was used in very large numbers in Poland and achieved rapid penetrations against lightly armed opponents. Although it was undoubtedly a fast vehicle, it suffered from very thin armour and an inadequate main gun.

A Pz.Kpfw.II rolls past anti-tank gunners on a road near the Bzura River in early September 1939. This Pak35/36 anti-tank gun may well have been used to remove enemy resistance, before the Panzers moved forward. This type of anti-tank support was of decisive importance for the preparation and the successful conduct of a tank attack, and was used extensively in the Panzer divisions throughout the war.

21

Stationary Pz.Kpfw.I's in early September 1939. Prior to making any more advances these vehicles are probably waiting for support. Surprisingly in Poland, support vehicles were a vital asset to the Panzer divisions and were a major contribution to the success on the battlefield. Even unopposed movement, there was extreme wear and tear to the Panzers. These machines were also not very reliable and needed frequent repairs.

As a column of horse drawn transport moves along the side of a road, in the opposite direction trundles two Pz.Kpfw.IV Ausf.D mounting its powerful short-barrelled 7.5cm KwK L/24. As early as the Polish campaign this tank had quickly demonstrated its superiority on the battlefield.

Two Pz.Kpfw.I`s along a dusty road in Poland in mid-September 1939. Note the Panzer crewman raising a signal baton. These batons were used to direct traffic, signalling to other tanks. In this instance, the commander of this tank has given the go ahead to proceed ahead.

Polish peasants watch by the side of the road as German armoured vehicles arrive on the outskirts of their town. An Sd.Kfz.263 armoured radio vehicle has come to a stop. This vehicle was equipped with a long radio set and was usually seen in signal units and in Corps and army headquarters.

Moving forward into action a Pz.Kpfw.II passes through a village chasing retreating enemy forces. Following this successful armoured spearhead are two light Horch cross-country cars. Within a few days of the German invasion of Poland the Panzer divisions were fighting an almost unopposed thrust east, against a disorganized jumble of retreating Polish units.

An interesting photograph showing an Sd.Kfz.263 radio vehicle with three Sd.Kfz.221 light armoured cars parked on the road to Sochaczev in mid-September 1939. These vehicles belong to the 1.SS.*Leibstandarte*-Division, which supported the 4.Panzer-Divisions, advance towards Lodz. Initially the advance went extremely well until confronted by strong enemy resistance in the town of Pabianice.

A German crossing point has been established on the banks of the Vistula River on 10 September 1939. A motorcyclist combination can be seen crossing the makeshift wooden bridge that was hastily constructed by pioneers only a day earlier. The main rivers in Poland, generally flowing from south to north of the country formed a natural barrier against an east-west assault. Polish engineers immediately set to work blowing many of the bridges to hinder the armoured advance.

An Sd.Kfz.263 armoured radio vehicle belonging to the 1.SS *Leibstandarte*-Division makes its way slowly through the destroyed town of Sochaczev. In order to move along the main road SS troops have obviously used the vehicle as support. The fighting for the town was particularly bitter with many German soldiers killed and wounded trying to capture it.

A column of Horch light cross-country vehicles towing Pak 35/36 anti-tank guns have halted at the roadside during the 4.Panzer-Divisions drive on Warsaw in early September 1939. This photograph vividly illustrates the lack of armoured vehicles during the campaign with Horch cars being utilised to pull armour. In fact, much of the logistics still relied heavily on horses to tow supplies and artillery.

A stationary Sd.Kfz.263 armoured radio vehicle. These eight-wheeled turretless vehicles were used extensively in Poland and were particularly useful as armoured support against strong Polish resistance. In order to reduce the amount of losses all traces of the painted white cross on the hull of the vehicle, intended as a distinguishing mark to avoid friendly fire, appears to have been omitted to reduce the chances of Polish anti-tank gunners.

Another piece of armour to be widely used during the Polish campaign was the light 7.5cm Infantry Gun 18. Although antiquated, it was able to put out of action an enemy vehicle without too much trouble.

A variety of armoured vehicles, including a halftrack advance along a congested road. One prime mover can be seen towing a 15cm sFH18 heavy field howitzer. In order to neutralise enemy resistance and allow the infantry or a Panzer division to continue its drive these heavy field guns could be brought up to the front lines to engage the enemy rapidly.

A prime mover is towing a 15cm sFH18 heavy field howitzer across a pontoon bridge in eastern Poland. The gun crew can be seen clearly occupying the seats inside the vehicle. Much of the transportation of this type of gun was done by halftrack instead of horse. This enabled crews to work effectively and minimized the distance between artillery and advanced Panzer units.

Here a 15cm sFH18 heavy field howitzer opens fire at enemy positions. The battery officer can be seen raising his hand signalling for the gun crew to fire. Before an armoured attack, artillery crews concentrated on the enemy in the assembly areas, unleashing their firepower. Artillery fire was heaviest where Panzers would be unable to operate, but from where they could engage effectively.

An infantry support vehicle tows a 7.5cm Infantry Gun 18 along a road. For the needs of the infantry in 1939 this field gun actually had an excessively great initial velocity of its shells, and the trajectory was not variable enough.

A column of vehicles including two Pz.Kpfw.I`s drive along one of the many terrible road systems in which armoured vehicles had to travel. Many roads were often sandy tracks, and virtually inaccessible to horse-drawn transport. Had the invasion been postponed any later than September, both infantry and Panzer divisions alike would have experienced logistical problems due to the autumn rains.

A soldier ensures that one of the 15cm sFH18 heavy field howitzers is secured prior to its long journey by rail back to Germany. Moving armour by rail would become a common requirement by the Panzer divisions. It would enable them to move from one front to another quickly and effectively without wear and tear.

An interesting scene showing various support vehicles and motorcycle combinations spread out in a ploughed field. Foliage has been draped over two of the motorcycle combinations, obviously to minimise the risk of aerial attack.

A German soldier armed with an MG 34 machine gun sits along a roadside as a Pz.Kpfw.III passes by. The MG 34 was a formidable weapon of war and was the main infantry-support weapon that first saw action in Poland. A well-sighted, well-hidden and well-supplied MG 34 could hold up an entire attacking regiment.

Chapter Three

Western Campaign

Just eight months after the defeat of Poland the *Panzerwaffe* had expanded to ten Panzer divisions with some 2,400 Panzers. This Panzer force was to be used to wage a war in the West against the Low Countries and France. For Hitler's western offensive he had assembled some 117 divisions, including a reserve of 42 infantry divisions. The remainder of the units were distributed between Army Group A and B, commanded by General Gerd von Rundstedt and General Fedor von Bock.

Army Group A had the main task of destroying the weak defences of the Ardennes region and driving to up to the Channel Sea, in the process encircling and smashing the allied armies. The army group consisted of 45$^1/_2$ divisions, of which were seven Panzer. Army Group B consisted of 29$^1/_2$ divisions, of which were three Panzer. The army group had the task of attacking Holland and northern Belgium to drive out the French 1st Army along the Dyle river line, pushing them back into France, and annihilating them in the process.

For the Western campaign the *Panzerwaffe* had managed to muster together some 2,702 tanks. In total there were 640 Pz.Kpfw.I's, 825 Pz.Kpfw.II's, 456 Pz.Kpfw.III's, 366 Pz.Kpfw.IV's, 151 Pz.Kpfw.35(t)'s and 264 Pz.Kpfw.38(t)'s. The reserves number some 160 vehicles to replace the combat losses and 135 Pz.Kpfw.I's and Pz.Kpfw.III's had been converted into armoured command tanks, which resulted in them losing their armament.

The vehicles that had been distributed among the ten Panzer divisions were not distributed according to formation of the battles they were supposed to perform. The 1.Panzer-Division, 2.Panzer-Division and 10.Panzer-Division each contained 30 Pz.Kpfw.I's, 100 Pz.Kpfw.II's, 90 Pz.Kpfw.III's and 56 Pz.Kpfw.IV's.

The 6.Panzer-Division, 7.Panzer-Division and 8.Panzer-Division consisted of 10 Pz.Kpfw.I's, 40 Pz.Kpfw.II's, 132 Pz.Kpfw.35 (t)'s or Pz.Kpfw.38 (t)'s and 36 Pz.Kpfw.IV's. A further 19 Pz.Kpfw.35 (t)'s were added to the 6.Panzer-Division due to the compliment of a battery of sIG mechanised infantry guns.

The 3.Panzer-Division, 4.Panzer-Division and 5.Panzer-Division each consisted of 140 Pz.Kpfw.I's, 110 Pz.Kpfw.II's, 50 Pz.Kpfw.III's and 24 Pz.Kpfw.IV's.

In addition to the main armoured vehicles that made up the Panzer divisions, various other types of armoured units were to take part in the Western campaign. There were for instance four independent Sturmartillerie batteries, each of six *Sturmegeschütz* (StuG) III assault guns. This was a specially developed vehicle armed with a 7.5cm howitzer bolted on the chassis of a Pz.Kpfw.III. Apart from the new StuG.III there were also two types of independent specialist anti-armour units deployed for action. There were five *Panzerjäger* companies equipped with a 4.7cm Pak auf Pz.Kpfw.I, which was known as the Marder.I tank destroyer. The Marder.I had a Czech 4.7cm anti-tank mounted on the chassis of a Pz.Kpfw.I. This vehicle provided at the time ample mobile anti-tank support for the infantry divisions.

To support the advancing Panzer divisions there was a single company of ten-8.8cm Flak 18 *auf Zugkraftwagen's*. These 8.8cm flak guns were mounted on the chassis of an armoured Sd.Kfz.7 half-track in order to give much needed firepower support against the thickly armoured British Matilda and French Char B tanks.

When the attack was finally unleashed against the West in the early hours of 10 May 1940 it caught the allied forces completely by surprise. Similar to the tactics used against Poland a point for the armoured spearhead was chosen. Here it would concentrate on this central point and the weight of firepower with supporting units would be used to overwhelm the enemy. Once a breach had been made the rest of the Panzer division would rush through the gap into the enemy areas. The tanks would continue to reap fire and devastation and drive deep inside the enemy lines, whilst infantry and artillery would deal with the pockets of resistance. The anti-tank gunners would set up a defensive screen to protect the areas already captured by the armoured spearhead of Panzer division. This type of concept was fairly simple, but was very effective and advanced at the time. It was used repeatedly throughout the Western campaign with devastating results. Panzer commanders had proved in Poland that a deep rapid advance into the enemy lines provided its own defence. In Holland, Belgium and France this strategy of attack was of breathtaking audacity.

Against Holland and Belgium the Panzer divisions launched their offensives with powerful concentration of armour. Without any real opposition, this arm of the attack mercilessly cut through the meagre allied defences and tore into France with tactical superiority. Within three days the Germans had reached the river Meuse, which was one of the great obstacles confronting the invaders. The river was quickly crossed in three places and at some points was confronted by heavy resistance. Once the Panzer divisions had crossed the journey ahead was ideal tank country. In places the drive had been so rapid that extending back from the Meuse nearly to the Rhine, crowded 25 divisions of the supporting infantry.

The most significant advance on the Western Front was made by the 7.Panzer-Division commanded by General Erwin Rommel. Nicknamed the '*Spook Division*', for it's speed, Rommel's armoured might drove through the lightly defended areas of

France and used speed and weight of fire to surprise and overwhelm the withdrawing enemy. This Panzer division had become the first to cross the Meuse. Once across they made an all out assault towards the town of Arras, engaging strong British and French forces on the way.

General Heinz Guderian's amazing sweep from the Meuse was a master stroke and exemplified Blitzkrieg tactics using Panzer divisions in the most lethal efficient form. His tanks drove at breakneck speed, frequently covering some 50 miles a day and far outstripping the supporting units of the division. By 20 May Guderian reached Amiens. The Allies to the north and south were now torn apart. Four days later, as the British Expeditionary Force fled onto the breaches at Dunkirk, Hitler decided to make a controversial order and halt the tanks sitting outside the town. This Führer order undoubtedly saved the massacre of thousands of British and French troops as they evacuated the beaches.

In less than three weeks the enemy had been completely defeated. On 20 June, after just six weeks of war France agreed to surrender. The Panzer divisions had once again played a crucial part in the victory. The allies had anticipated a re-run of the First World War plan and distributed their forces accordingly. They had failed to recognize the real potential of the tank, and as a consequence they were quickly overrun and fell back in confusion and panic.

With the war in the West won and with a sense of invincibility in everyone's mind, Hitler was already looking to undertake an even bolder gamble.

Early on 10 May 1940, the invasion of the Low Countries began. Here in this photograph are a group of prime movers with 15cm sFH18 heavy field howitzers on tow. They are part of the 9.Panzer-Division and parked in a captured Dutch town near the Maas River. Within three days of the invasion the 9.Panzer-Division had arrived on the outskirts of Rotterdam. By 15 May 1940 the city fell, along with shattered remnants of the entire Dutch Army.

Driving through a Belgium town, a heavily camouflaged prime mover towing what is probably an 8.8cm Flak 39. This was the most famous anti-aircraft gun of World War Two and was specifically designed for a dual role. It possessed a genuine anti-tank capability and was used extensively in the West against both ground and aerial targets. The driver of the prime mover is attached to a *Luftwaffe* flak detachment.

Various vehicles move along a congested road in an assembly point area in Holland. Two prime movers are towing heavy field howitzers. Already thousands of tons of equipment and supplies had poured through into Holland and Belgium, bolstering the strength of the infantry and Panzer divisions as they hurtled towards the French frontier.

Pioneers with their bridge building sections halt inside a decimated town. This photograph was taken on 11 May 1940 near the Meuse River. Later that day these portable bridges were slung across the river to allow the 3. and 4.Panzer-Divisions to cross. The Belgium Army had regarded the rivers and canals as a major obstacle to German motorised units. But the Panzers still proved adept at negotiating the water obstacles, even when heavily defended.

A Pz.Kpfw.IV has come to a stop on a road near the French border. This armoured vehicle was more than capable of knocking out most potential opposition. However, the tank was not as heavily armoured as some of its allied opponents. Nonetheless the Pz.Kpfw.IV achieved many successes in the West and was feared by its enemy.

A variety of Panzers consisting of Pz.Kpfw.II`s, III`s, IV`s, and a Pz.Kpfw.38 (t) are strategically spread out in a field. They have probably halted in order to allow the support vehicles to catch up with them. This enables the tank crews to pause for a much-needed respite and attend to any external repairs or adjustments to their vehicles.

Although a versatile armoured vehicle across varied terrain, halftracks were persistently prone to mechanical problems. They were also liable to develop engine faults in water as this photograph vividly illustrates. It is more than likely that the driver has flooded the engine compartment and is unable to restart the engine.

Various armoured vehicles including Horch light cross-country cars are parked next to a French church. By 21 May 1940 German armour had demonstrated its ability to penetrate enemy lines, all the while bypassing strong points and holding the enemy at bay until their own lines of communication could be restored.

The Horch light cross-country car was used extensively in the Panzer divisions throughout the war. They were not only utilised to carry personnel from one part of the front to another, they were utilized for a number of important roles, even towing armour up to the front lines. Officers too sometimes travelled in them and they were even pressed into service to carry wounded back to field hospitals.

Pz.Kpfw.I, II, III and IV's can be seen halted inside a newly captured French town. Evidence of some heavy fighting is apparent by the charred remains of two buildings. By 21 May 1940 General Heinz Guderian's Panzers secured a bridgehead on the Somme. He then advanced at speed on Boulogne and Calais.

A light infantry support vehicle follows another vehicle towing a 3.7cm Pak35/36 anti-tank gun. This anti-tank weapon proved relatively successful on the Western Front in 1940 and was able to quite easily penetrate 48mm of vertical homogenous armour.

A motley collection of support vehicles inside a captured French town. With surrounding buildings and roads almost intact, there appears to be little sign of defensive action in this area, suggesting the allies had withdrawn very quickly to escape the powerful spearheads of the Panzer divisions.

A motorcycle battalion being transported on board a railway flatcar destined for the frontlines. Although the *Panzerwaffe* put hundreds of soldiers on motorcycles, motorcycles were quite often unsuited to modern warfare, except for dispatch riders. On bad road surfaces they were totally useless, and riders were vulnerable to small arms fire and mantraps.

In a drastic attempt to contain the armoured spearheads of the Panzer divisions and prevent the crossing of vital rivers, the allies blew a number of bridges during their retreat. For this reason, the construction of pontoon bridges was widely used. Here in this photograph a 15cm sFH 18 heavy field howitzer is being prepared to be moved across the bridge.

On the road to Dunkirk a column of support vehicles has halted at the roadside. A motorcyclist dressed in the familiar leather motorcycle coat wanders over to a group of comrades parked with their Kfz.15 light cross-country vehicle.

A Pz.Kpfw.IV hurtles along a dusty road in northern France. It seemed nothing on earth could prevent the mighty Panzer divisions from crushing the allied troops that were now being driven along the Channel coast. On 22 May 1940, the 1.Panzer-Division were moving in to attack Calais, whilst the 2.Panzer-Division, was arriving on the outskirts of Boulogne.

Swinging north from the town of Abbeville a column of prime movers towing 15cm sFH heavy field guns is on the road to Boulogne on 21 May 1940. These vehicles are part of the 2.Panzer-Division. Within twenty-four hours these guns would be pounding British positions defending the seacoast port, allowing infantry and armour to pour into the town and fight street by street.

Engineers prepare for the crossing of support vehicles on a hastily erected pontoon bridge. This bridge has been lashed together with inflatable boats. For river crossings under fire, inflatable boats were used for assault, and then relegated to bridging or ferrying.

An Sd.Kfz.251 moves across a French field. This vehicle is newly fitted with the MG 34 machine gun. Although this vehicle was first used as a troop transporter that could deliver and drop troops at the edge of the battlefield, during the Western Campaign, halftracks mounted Panzergrenadiers moved alongside armour and provided them with valuable support.

A soldier poses for the camera in front of an Sd.Kfz.7 prime mover during the Western Campaign in May 1940. The Sd.Kfz.7 was used extensively in the Panzer divisions throughout the war to carry infantry to the battlefield. They were also used to tow artillery and armour that had developed mechanical problems.

Following in the wake of the armoured drive through France, a number of support vehicles cross a pontoon bridge. Despite the shortages of vehicles in the Panzer divisions, during this period of the war there were no less than 100 different types of commercial lorries in army service.

An Sd.Kfz.7 prime mover towing a 15cm sFH heavy field howitzer on the road to Dunkirk in May 1940. For the immediate needs of battle, the Panzer divisions relied much on these heavy artillery pieces and the way in which they were transported and positioned in the field was more than reason enough why artillery needed tracked vehicles, rather than slow, cumbersome horse-drawn transport.

During Hitler`s famous halt order outside Dunkirk on 24 May 1940, a group of motorcyclists take full opportunity of the situation to relax and play a game of cards. Two of the soldiers are wearing the standard motorcycle waterproof coat. They are wearing aviator goggles, which were standard issue to all motorcycle units.

A dejected line of captured French prisoners being force-marched along a road in northern France. These prisoners are just a few of the enemy forces that were trapped in pockets as the powerful Panzer divisions pushed forward. Passing them in the opposite direction is a convoy of trucks, transport vehicles and motorcyclists.

A Sturmegeschütz (StuG) III self-propelled assault gun making its debut in France. These vehicles saw limited service in the campaign in the West, but soon proved a valuable infantry support vehicle. Full production commenced in July 1940. The main armament was a short-barrelled 7.5cm StuK 37 L/24 gun.

A Henschel truck with a full compliment of flak crew inside tows an 8.8cm heavy anti-aircraft gun. Even during the Western Campaign the 8.8cm flak gun demonstrated outstanding anti-tank capabilities and attributed greatly to the success of the Panzer divisions.

A group of soldiers with a parked Pz.Kpfw.III outside a petrol service station somewhere in northern France in late May 1940. A number of tanks had advanced so far ahead of the supporting column that frequently they ran out of fuel or had to halt to wait for vital supplies.

During the early evening of 14 June 1940 the first German troops, men of the 9.Infantry-Division, entered Paris. Two days later a victory parade took place in the French capital. Here in this photograph a number of light support vehicles and motorcycle combination can be seen in front of the Eiffel Tower.

Chapter Four

The Balkans

Following the defeat of France in June 1940 Hitler became increasingly uneasy about the state of the Axis position in the Balkans and wasted no time drawing up plans with his army commanders to invade it. By mid-December 1940, 'Operation Marita', the codename for the invasion of Greece, was almost prepared. During the following three months German divisions were moved to southern Romania.

On 6 April 1941, German forces simultaneously attacked Yugoslavia and Greece. In Yugoslavia, following heavy bombardments of Belgrade, German infantry supported by the Panzerwaffe moved across the Yugoslavian frontier. Once again the Panzerwaffe were able to test their expertise on the battlefields of Europe.

For the invasion of Yugoslavia the plan of attack was divided between the 12th Army commanded by Field Marshal List, the 2nd Army commanded by General Maximilian von Weichs, and General Ewald von Kleist's Panzer Group 1.

Altogether the *Panzerwaffe* deployed the 4, 12, 19.Panzer-Divisions into reserve, whilst the 2nd Army consisted of the 8.and 14.Panzer-Divisions. Both these Panzer divisions attacked in the general direction of Belgrade between the Drava and Sava Rivers. The terrain between the two rivers was considered ideal for armoured warfare, and no serious obstacles hindered the drive.

Field Marshal List's 12th Army, which consisted of the 2. and 9.Panzer-Divisions had been assembled in Bulgaria for the purpose of executing the attack in the Balkans. The 16.Panzer-Division remained in army group reserves. Kleist's Panzer Group 1 consisted of 5. and 11.Panzer-Divisions. These Panzer divisions were forced to negotiate some formidable mountain roads before reaching their objective.

In their familiar Blitzkrieg style three separate ground forces converged on Belgrade from different directions. The Panzer Group jumped off from its assembly area northwest of Sofiya. Crossing the frontier near Pirot, the 16.Panzer-Korps, spearheaded by the 11.Panzer Division, followed by the 5. Panzer, 294.Infantry, and 4.Mountain Divisions, advanced in a northwesterly direction toward Nis. Despite unfavourable weather, numerous road blocks, and tough resistance by the Yugoslav 5th Army, the 11.Panzer-Division, effectively supported by strong artillery and Luftwaffe forces, quickly gained ground and broke through the enemy lines on the first day of the attack. Within hours leading German tanks rumbled into Nis and immediately continued their drive toward Belgrade.

In 2nd Army the 8. and 14.Panzer-Divisons had also made very good progress despite poor roads and bad weather conditions. Enemy pockets were quickly mopped up and the 8.Panzer-Division drove on in the direction of the capital via Osijok, where the roads became even worse. Whilst the 14.Panzer-Division drove towards its objective of Zagreb, the state capital of Croatia, the 8.Panzer-Division pushed forward, and by 13 April had reached the outskirts of Belgrade. The 2.SS.Motorized-Infantry-Division had already arrived there a day earlier. During the night the 8.Panzer-Division rolled into Belgrade, occupied the city centre, and hoisted the Swastika flag. At dawn the 11.Panzer-Division began to roll into the Yugoslav capital.

Two days earlier on 11 April lead tanks of the 14. Panzer-Division reached the outskirts of Zagreb, after having covered a distance of almost 100 miles in one day. In some areas surrounding the city Croat troops refused to fight and either deserted or surrendered. So rapid was the advance of the Panzer division that its radio communications with corps and army were temporarily interrupted. Reconnaissance aircraft had to be dispatched to ascertain its exact location and chart its progress. When the 14. Panzer-Division entered Zagreb from the northeast it was welcomed by a cheering pro-German population. During the drive on the city more than 15,000 prisoners were taken. Among the 300 officers were twenty-two generals, including the commanders of the Yugoslav 1st Army Group and 7th Army.

For the 14.Panzer-Division its journey did not end with the capture of Zagreb. The following day the division pulled out and was ordered to spearhead the drive on Sarajevo from the west. The eastern pursuit force, under the command of the Panzer Group.1, was composed of six divisions, with the 8.Panzer-Division leading the drive toward Sarajevo from the east. The 8 Panzer-Division wasted no time and sped eastward toward Sarajevo. One armoured division combed out the sector south of Belgrade, while two infantry divisions cleared the industrial region in and around Nis. The 8. Panzer-Division led the way toward Sarajevo, closely followed by two motorized infantry divisions that were driving hard toward the heart of Yugoslavia.

The speed of the Panzer divisions was truly amazing and between 14 and 15 April, thousands of prisoners were taken. North of Nis the Germans captured 7,000. Around Uzice, 40,000 were captured, in and around Zvornik 30,000 went into captivity, and in Doboj another 6,000 fell to the on-rushing armoured forces.

On 15 April both pursuit groups of 2nd.Army closed in on Sarajevo. As the two Panzer divisions entered the city simultaneously from west and east, the Yugoslav 2nd Army, whose headquarters was in Sarajevo, capitulated. Leaving only security detachments in the city to await the arrival of the German forces.

The Yugoslav campaign had been won. The Panzer divisions that had fought their way through mountainous terrain in northwestern Yugoslavia had accomplished their missions relatively well. After the initial penetrations had been achieved, powerful armoured wedges exploited the situation by breaking through at various points and swiftly moving deep into the enemy rear. It was here that German motorised equipment surpassed all expectations by covering great distances with lightning speed against antiquated enemy forces, winding roads and through narrow, treacherous mountain passes. There can be no doubt that it was the rapid thrusts of the Panzer divisions across the mountains that broke the back of enemy resistance and spelled the early doom of the Yugoslav Army.

In Greece, the course of the campaign had also developed exactly as predicted. The invasion had in fact started simultaneously with the assault on Yugoslavia. In two-days fighting, 6 – 7 April, General Kleist's Panzer Divisions had broken the resistance of the Yugoslavs in Macedonia and forced the Greek defenders of the Metaxas Line. Kleist's Panzer divisions then moved rapidly westward towards where the British were hastily preparing defensive positions between Mount Olympus and Salonika. The 5. Panzer-Division struck hard and soon smashed an open road to Mount Olympus. On 13 April the 2. Panzer-Division bypassed the doomed Mount Olympus and made an all out drive south. The 9. Panzer-Division also made a series of strong attacks, and by 14 April reached the town of Kozani. For three long hours armour supported by artillery and infantry attacked British positions in the surrounding hills until the town finally fell.

The Greeks capitulated on 23 April and the British abandoned positions in and around Thermopylae the next day, pulling back into the Peloponnese where the Royal Navy subsequently evacuated what was left of the worn out and badly depleted forces.

The success in the Balkans was undoubtedly attributed to the use of the Panzer divisions over supposedly impassable terrain. The operations that the Panzerwaffe employed both in Yugoslavia and Greece were models of great planning, precision and efficiency with armour systematically carving up the opposition and annihilating piecemeal. But there was a price to be paid for the victory in the Balkans. It seemed that wear and tear, especially to tracked vehicles, had necessitated drastic measures for almost every vehicle to be taken off the road for a three-week overhaul. This was a lesson to be learnt for the constant use of armoured vehicles in harsh climates or difficult and unfavourable terrain. It was undoubtedly a lesson, which was repeated, time and again in the vast expanses of Russia.

An Sd.Kfz.7 prime mover together with support vehicles during the opening phase of the Balkans campaign on 6 April 1941. These vehicles belong to 8.Panzer-Division whose objective it was to attack in the direction of the city of Belgrade. Although the speed of the Panzer divisions in the Balkans was rapid, vehicles in some units experienced mechanical problems, which consequently slowed the advance. Unfavourable weather and terrain also hindered movement in areas.

One of the first Yugoslav towns to be occupied by the 8.Panzer-Division in the border region. In front of a building, which is flying the national flag, stands an Sd.Kfz.7 towing what appears to be a well-camouflaged artillery piece. Straw seems to be covering the entire roof of the prime mover and the gun in order to minimise the possibility of aerial attack.

A column of heavily laden Pz.Kpfw.III`s from the 46.Panzer-Korps during it's furious drive on Belgrade in early April 1941. The crew have stowed a number of items over the engine deck, including supplies and rolled-up canvas sheeting. Note the spare wheels attached to the rear for additional armoured protection.

Pz.Kpfw.III`s move through a Yugoslav town, which appears to have been captured without a fight. As with the previous campaigns, the Pz.Kpfw.III demonstrated its effectiveness at over-running enemy positions with speed and manoeuvrability, and used its gun as artillery against forward enemy columns with devastating effect.

As the Panzer divisions simultaneously attacked Yugoslavia and Greece, armoured units were able to once again test their expertise at outflanking and cutting off the enemy. This photograph shows captured British forces in Greece hitching a lift onboard a Pz.Kpfw.IV. A group of motorcyclists are obviously preparing to follow the convoy of prisoners as they are taken to hastily erected PoW camps.

A variety of armoured vehicles have occupied a village square. They include two Pz.Kpfw.III`s, a light radio car, Opel Blitz truck, and a number of other vehicles. This photograph was taken on 8 April 1941.

Crossing a pontoon bridge is an Sd.Kfz.7 towing an 8.8cm Flak gun. German pioneer units were well practised in constructing pontoon bridges as rapidly as possible. In order to cross vital rivers and other obstacles the Panzer divisions relied heavily on the pioneers.

An Sd.Kfz.7 towing a 15cm sFH heavy field howitzer passes over a river on a wooden bridge built by German pioneers to carry heavier armour. Note the pontoon bridge erected alongside the wooden bridge. This was built in order carry lighter loads in the Panzer divisions.

Two Pz.Kpfw.III`s rumble past a column of marching *Gebirgsjäger* (mountain troops) belonging to the 7.Gebirgs-Division. When the Balkan campaign began, the mountain division moved south, taking part in the brief campaign against Greece and in particular the smashing of the Metaxas line supported by General Kleist`s Panzer divisions.

A motorcyclist comes to a complete stop on a road with other vehicles north of Belgrade. The Panzer divisions were dependent upon all the good roads in the Balkans.

A Krupp-Protz Kfz.81 armoured vehicle is towing a PaK 35/36 flak gun across some rough terrain on the border with Yugoslavia in early April 1941. It is more than likely that these troops have been on military exercises and training manoeuvres prior to the Balkans campaign, as they are all wearing the battle practice helmet bands.

An Sd.Kfz.223 light armoured car leads a column of Sd.Kfz.221's through a town, watched by bewildered civilians at the roadside. This vehicle was armed with a 2cm KwK 30 cannon and co-axial 7.92mm MG 34 mounted in a 10-sided, open-topped rotating turret. A wire-mesh hood protected the turret top from grenade attacks.

Rear echelon troops of the 9.Panzer-Division on the Bulgarian border with Greece in early April 1941. It had been Field-Marshal Lists' 12th Army, consisting of the 2. and 9.Panzer-Divisions that had crossed over the Bulgarian frontier into Greece to begin a simultaneous attack of the Balkans.

A pause during the furious drive through the Balkans. Here a group of soldiers relax and eat their rations by the roadside. In front of the support vehicle two motorcyclists can be seen with their motorcycle combination, wearing their distinctive loose fitting, rubberized coats and aviator goggles.

A number of vehicles belonging to an unidentified Panzer division have pulled into a town somewhere in the Balkans. Among the various halftracks towing anti-tank guns there is an infantry truck that can be seen carrying PoWs.

Support vehicles inside a town. Preparing for action relied heavily on trucks and many civilian armoured vehicles for transport and supply. Maintaining the momentum of a Panzer division's advance was vital and was the main artery to the success on the battlefield.

A Pz.Kpfw.III has halted inside a forest. The troops appear to have hitched a lift on board the vehicle. To maintain the speed of the armoured spearhead, accompanying infantry were carried into battle on the tanks and other armoured vehicles.

A Pz.Kpfw.III Ausf.E belonging to an unidentified Panzer regiment attached to the 2.Panzer-Division in Greece. All the crew are wearing the familiar black Panzer uniform and field cap. The colour was primarily designed to hide oil and other stains when working with armoured vehicles.

Moving along a dusty road during operations in Greece, a column of horse-drawn transport passes a Pz.Kpfw.III that has evidently been knocked out of action and has extensive fire damage. One of the crewmembers wearing just his black Panzer trousers can be seen walking away from his disabled machine.

An Sd.Kfz.10 halftrack crosses a bridge in Greece towing an ammunition trailer. The body of the vehicle was entered by climbing over the side, and the interior could be covered from the weather by a fold down canopy and side curtains with clear windows.

The death rate amongst Panzer crews was extremely high. Here in this photograph a crewman pays his last respects to the crew of a Pz.Kpfw.III that were killed during operations in Greece. Note the tank cupola and track link either side of the national flag draped over the grave.

A Pz.Kpfw.III Ausf.G/H moves across some rocky terrain, and following behind is a light Horch cross-country car. Note the soldiers with their short-handled folding entrenching tools. It appears that a number of vehicles have experienced some problems negotiating the uneven terrain, and the drivers have required the soldiers to move some of the larger obstacles out of the way.

A long line of Horch cross-country cars and an Sd.Kfz.10 halftrack towing a Pak 35/36 anti-tank gun move steadily southwards towards the Greek peninsula. Within three weeks of the Balkan campaign the Panzer and infantry divisions of the *Wehrmacht* and *Waffen-SS* had occupied the Balkans.

A 3.7cm anti-tank gun mounted on the rear of an artillery tractor in front of the Acropolis following the defeat of Greece in late April 1941. Note the tactical sign painted in white on the left mudguard, indicating that it is the first flak gun in the battery.

Chapter Five

Barbarossa

For the invasion of Russia, code-named Barbarossa, the German Army assembled some three million men, divided into a total of 105 infantry divisions and 32 Panzer divisions. There were 3,332 tanks, over 7,000 artillery pieces, 60,000 motor vehicles and 625,000 horses. This force was distributed into three German army groups: Army Group North, commanded by Field Marshal Wilhelm Ritter von Leeb, had assembled his forces in East Prussia on the Lithuanian frontier. His *Panzergruppe*, which provided the main spearhead for the advance on Leningrad, consisted of 812 tanks. These were divided among the 1, 6 and 8.Panzer-Divisions, 3, 36.Motorised-Infantry-Division and the SS.Motorised-Division '*Totenkopf*', which formed the *Panzergruppe* reserve.

Army Group Centre, commanded by Field Marshal Fedor von Bock, assembled on the 1939 Polish/Russian frontier, both north and south of Warsaw. Bock's force consisted of 42 infantry divisions of the 4th and 9th Armies and *Panzergruppen II* and *III*. This army contained the largest number of German infantry and Panzer divisions in all three army groups. In *Panzergruppen II* there were some 930 tanks alone distributed between the 3, 4, 10, 17, and 18.Panzer-Divisions, the 10, and 29.Motorised-Infantry-Divisions, the SS.Motorised-Division '*Das Reich*' and the elite Motorised Infantry Regiment '*Grossdeutschland.*'

The second *Panzergruppe* of Army Group Centre, *Panzergruppe III*, contained 840 tanks and consisted of 7, 12, 19, and 20.Panzer-Divisions, 14 and 18.Motorised-Infantry-Divisions.

Army Group South, commanded by Field Marshal Gerd von Rundstedt was deployed down the longest stretch of border with Russia. The front, reaching from central Poland to the Black Sea, was held by one *Panzergruppe*, three German and two Rumanian armies, plus a Hungarian motorised corps, under German command.

Panzergruppe I provided the armoured support for Army Group South's advance into the Ukraine. It consisted of some 750 tanks which were distributed between 9, 13, 14, 16.Panzer-Divisions, the SS Motorised Divisions, '*Leibstandarte Adolf Hitler*' and '*Wiking*'. The 25.Motorised-Infantry-Division formed the *Panzergruppe* reserve.

Although the bulk of the Pz.Kpfw.I's and Pz.Kpfw.II's had formed the main tank strength of the Panzer divisions in the Polish and French campaigns, more than half the tank strength participating in 'Barbarossa' were still light tanks of German or Czech manufacture. A total of 3,332 German tanks stood poised for the largest military invasion in history.

The Panzer divisions' main armour consisted of: 410 Pz.Kpfw.I's, 746 Pz.Kpfw.II's, 149 Pz.Kpfw. 35(t) s, 623 Pz.Kpfw. 38(t) s, 965 Pz.Kpfw. III's, and 439 Pz.Kpfw.IV's. This armoured force had to rely on obsolete light tanks to provide the armoured punch.

For the Russian offensive the Panzer divisions had been slightly modified in armoured firepower. They had been in fact diluted in strength in order to form the deployment of more divisions. The planners thought that by concentrating a number of Panzer divisions together they were able to achieve a massive local superiority.

These new Panzer divisions contained one tank regiment of two, sometimes three *abteilungen* totalling some 150-200 tanks; two motorised rifle (*schützen*) regiments, each of two battalions, whose infantry were carried in armoured halftracks or similar vehicles, and a reconnaissance battalion of three companies (one motorcycle, two armoured car). The motorised infantry divisions accompanying the Panzer divisions in the *Panzergruppen* were similarly organised, but severely lacked armoured support. The divisional artillery comprised two field, one medium and one anti-tank regiment and an anti-aircraft battalion. These were all motorised and more than capable of keeping up with the fast moving pace of the Panzers.

During the early morning of 22 June 1941 the German Army finally unleashed the maelstrom that was Barbarossa. The Panzer divisions wasted no time and soon sliced through the bewildered Russian forces on every front. The ferocity and effectiveness of the Panzer divisions were so great that some of the Red Army forces they surrounded were gigantic. Groups of up to fifteen Russian divisions were trapped at a time and slowly and systematically annihilated in a hurricane of fire.

By 3 July the battle for the frontier was over and armoured and infantry units were pushing forward at breakneck speed achieving their tactical bounds. In Army Group North they had destroyed 43 Russian divisions within a week, and Army Group Centre boasted that the road to Moscow was penetrated to a depth of some 300km. In Army Group South the most advanced elements of the armoured spearhead were no more than 100km from the city of Kiev. Combat in Russia placed tremendous demands on the tank crews, but in the opening weeks of the offensive it had gone like clockwork. Even there Blitzkrieg tactics were working.

After a month of victorious progress, the German armies were fighting on a front 1,000 miles wide. The Panzer divisions had exploited the terrain and concerted such a series of hammer blows to the Red Army that it was only a matter of time before the campaign would be over. Yet in spite of these successes the Panzer divisions were thinly spread out. Although the armoured spearheads were still achieving rapid victories on all fronts, supporting units were not keeping pace with them. Consequently, it became increasingly difficult to keep the Panzers supplied with fuel.

And without fuel the drive would ground to a halt. Nevertheless, between June and late September 1941, the Panzer and motorised divisions were more or less unhindered by lack of supply, difficult terrain or bad weather conditions. However, on 6 October the first snowfall of the approaching winter was reported. It melted quickly, but turned the dirt roads into quagmires and rivers into raging torrents. The Russian Autumn with its heavy rain, sleet and snow had arrived. The Panzer divisions began to slow.

Already in Army Group Centre three infantry armies and three Panzer Groups had been employed in the drive on Moscow, code-named Operation Typhoon. Some 46 infantry divisions, 14 Panzer divisions, 8 motorised divisions and one motorised brigade were used for a three-pronged assault on the Russian capital. During the first week Typhoon had gone relatively well until the first snowfall. Russian resistance too resisted the advance with great courage and tenacity. By mid-October the weather continued to hamper German operations. Wheeled vehicles became stuck in a sea of mud and could only advance with the aid of tracked vehicles towing them. No preparations had been made for the winter and the Panzer divisions lacked the most basic supplies for cold weather. There were no chains available for towing vehicles, and no anti-freeze for the engine's coolant systems. Tank and infantrymen alike had no winter clothing either.

While the Panzers were immobilised the German infantry struggled forward overstretched and exhausted. Many armoured units too were down to half strength. Food for the Panzer divisions was now in short supply, ammunition and fuel was fast running out.

On 15 November the 3rd and 4th Panzer Armies unleashed an all out assault, which was intended to take them to Moscow. Two days later General Guderian's armoured force joined in the attack. Almost immediately they run into strong Russian resistance. In blizzards and temperatures, which fell to 30 degrees below zero, the exhausted Panzer divisions run out of fuel and ammunition, and were compelled to break off their attack within sight of Moscow. On 6 December all plans to capture Moscow in 1941 had to be abandoned.

By 22 December only 405 tanks were operational in front of the Russian capital with 780 out of action, but repairable. By the end of the year, the Germans reported the loss of 2,735 tanks plus 847 replacements since 22 June. Not even 1,400 operational and damaged tanks remained of the once powerful and proud Panzer divisions.

A Pz.Kpfw.IV rolls along a road during the opening phase of operation Barbarossa on 22 June 1941. During this early stage of the war, Panzer crews were still wearing their famous black Panzer uniforms. However, they soon found them completely unsuitable for camouflage purposes.

A motorcyclist with his BMW motorcycle wades through a muddy road following a freak summer rainstorm. Even during the summer periods in Russia the rain could suddenly turn a normal road into a quagmire. The Russian weather offered the Germans considerably greater challenges than they faced in both Poland and in Western Europe.

A Pz.Kpfw.IV Ausf.F1 passes along a typical Russian road in June 1941. The Ausf.F1 variant was the first up-armoured vehicle developed in response to heavy allied tanks during the Western Campaign. It was armed with a 7.5cm KwK 37 L/24 short-barrelled gun and was more than capable of dealing with Soviet KV-1 and T-34 tanks at short ranges. But by the time the Germans invaded Russia, there were only 548 Pz.Kpfw.IV Ausf.F1`s distributed among the Panzer divisions.

A motorcyclist reads a map. He is part of the medical personnel, which is indicated by the Red Cross painted on his sidecar combination. German medical personnel were kept very busy in Russia, especially during the winter periods.

Utilizing a hilltop, Panzer commanders watch the progress of their mighty armoured divisions pour across the Russian countryside to deliver the enemy a mighty blow. Despite this great show of power, the Panzer divisions were much weaker in numbers than their predecessors of 1939 and 1940.

A column of Pz.Kpfw.III`s move through a captured Russian town. Along the entire German front, the great armoured might of the *Panzerwaffe* pushed its way forward into action, deploying in extended order of advance and stretching over a distance of 11 – 16km.

A number of Sd.Kfz.263 armoured radio vehicles being transported to the front lines on board specially adapted railroad flatcars. These vehicles were equipped with a long-range radio set and were usually used by *Nachrichten* (signals) units and in *Korps* and *Armee* headquarters. Note the national flag draped over the front vehicle's antennae for aerial recognition.

Pz.Kpfw.II Ausf.F's roll along a dusty road watched by German mountain troops and local peasants. Despite the ineffectiveness of this tank on the front lines, this particular new model featured a homogenous 3.5cm-thick frontal plate, and the side armour had been increased to 3cm.

Prime movers with 8.8cm flak guns are being transported by rail to the Russian front during the early phase of Barbarossa. These vehicles belong to a *Wehrmacht Luftwaffe* flak detachment.

Soldiers preparing to mount a Pz.Kpfw.IV pose for the camera. During the Russian campaign it was common practice for supporting infantry to ride on board armoured vehicles to the front lines. This not only enabled troops to arrive at the forward edge of the battlefield quickly, but it also allowed soldiers the respite of long marches across the never-ending landscape of the Soviet Union.

On a training exercise during the summer of 1941. Smoke engulfs a Pz.Kpfw.IV, and a crew member can be seen escaping from the tank. In 1941 tank crews were generally highly trained and were given numerous drills and exercises on baling out of a knocked out vehicle. With ammunition stored on board in a real-life situation it was imperative that the Panzer be abandoned quickly and efficiently, for it could explode at any moment.

A Pz.Kpfw.III advances through a field. In the distance other armoured vehicles can be seen spread out in order to minimise the risk of losses to aerial attack. These armoured vehicles belong to the Panzer divisions of Army Group Centre during its drive on Moscow in 1941.

Rear units of a Panzer division pull into the captured town of Vitebsk in July 1941. Russian prisoners can be seen being marched off to their fate. Thousands of prisoners were taken in and around Vitebsk. Just six days later a massive encirclement around Smolensk saw the capture of some 300,000 Red Army troops.

An sFH 18 heavy artillery gun being pulled by a heavy artillery tractor. The artillery crew can be seen sitting in the back of the vehicle. The road system in Russia was very poor and the Panzer divisions relied heavily on tracked vehicles, even during the summer periods.

The crew of a halftrack prime mover watch one of their comrades lay out 15cm shells on to pieces of wood. The shells have been stored inside a specially adapted mobile bunker ready to be used against enemy targets at a moments notice.

Light Horch cross-country vehicles pass through one of the many destroyed towns and villages in western Russia during the summer of 1941. During this period the Panzer divisions continued to more or less go from one victory to another.

A Horch staff car has stopped inside a newly captured Russian town. The officer has stepped out from his vehicle and is conferring with a soldier holding a signals baton in his hand. A stationary motorcyclist armed with a 98k Mauser rifle is more than likely protecting the staff car.

A congested road somewhere in western Russia during the summer of 1941. A line of horse-drawn transport, armoured vehicles and a motorcycle combination has ground to a halt on one of the better road systems in the area. With the Soviet Air Force almost annihilated, aerial attacks against Panzer division columns were minimal.

Soldiers of an unidentified unit watch as a long line of Red Army prisoners are evacuated to the rear to a destination that can only be imagined. By September 1941 almost two million Russian soldiers had been captured. Victory now seemed to be beckoning for the German Army.

More armoured vehicles destined for the Eastern Front prepare to be moved out on railroad flat cars. By September 1941, the Panzer divisions were beginning to show signs of wear and tear. More replacement vehicles were needed to replace those that urgently required maintenance, but because there were so many that needed assistance in the field the Panzer divisions were compelled to carry on regardless.

A Krupp-Protz armoured vehicle towing a Pak 35/36 anti-tank gun leaves the frontier region of Poland for deployment in the East. By mid-1941, the Pak 35/36 anti-tank gun had become no match for a number of Russian tanks on the battlefield.

Two motorcyclists lend a hand to a flak crew, whose Sd.Kfz.7/1 halftrack has come under attack and been damaged as a consequence. The armoured vehicle is armed with a 2cm (Flak 30 anti-aircraft gun. Anti-aircraft defences came into prominence in September 1941, as the Soviet Air Force started to inflict heavy casualties.

One of the quickest and most effective forms of being transported from one battlefront to another was by rail. Here in this photograph a long column of light and heavy support vehicles wait for a transport train to take them to another part of the Eastern Front.

Light vehicles belonging to the famous 1.SS.Panzer-Division *Leibstandarte* in September 1941. This crack SS division were deeply embroiled in the battles in western Ukraine. The division's drive had been rapid in spite of meeting spirited resistance.

Vehicles towing heavy artillery negotiate a winding road on the edge of a forest. Great regions of western Russia were heavily forested and communications in the whole area were very poor. Panzer divisions depended upon small numbers of roads, radiating from East Prussia, Warsaw and going through narrow corridors of land to the principle cities of the Soviet Union.

A heavy field howitzer at the moment of firing as it hurls its shell miles into the enemy lines. Before an armoured attack, artillery crews concentrated on enemy tanks in the assembly areas, unleashing their firepower where anti-tank guns were suspected to be located.

A typical scene in Russia during the autumn of 1941, a column of support vehicles struggling along a road. Following continuous rainfall, the ground became extremely boggy and could easily reduce a dusty uneven road into a slough of mire. In western Russia the roads had not been constructed to carry the amount of traffic that now used them, and the surface began to break up under the strain.

Two Sd.Kfz.7 prime movers towing heavy field artillery make their way slowly through the snow. Two support vehicles carrying ammunition move along between them. There was little planning for winter operations in Russia, and by the time the first snow showers arrived, the front lines began to slow almost to a stop.

A group of soldiers pose for the camera in front of a Pz.Kpfw.II. Ausf.F during the first snow falls in Russia. They are all wearing gas mask canisters and greatcoats, except for the Panzer crewman standing at the end. As the artic temperatures dropped and the weather worsened the Panzer divisions would soon grind to a halt in the snow.

During the harsh winter in Russia a Pz.Kpfw.III has fallen victim to the extreme arctic conditions and appears to have fallen through ice. Infantry look on helpless. The shock of the first winter was considerable for the infantry and tank crews. Movement was made even worse by the terrain and lack of tracked vehicles.

A 15cm sFH 18 heavy field howitzer has turned over, probably whilst being towed by a prime mover on a slippery gradient in the deep snow. A group of soldiers can only examine the field piece, for they need specialist equipment to haul the gun carriage and bogey trailer back onto its wheels.

Chapter Six

The Afrika Korps

With the great achievements accomplished by the Panzer divisions in Europe, Mussolini was determined to follow in the footsteps of Hitler and decided to invade Egypt from the colony of Libya in September 1940. Vastly understrength, his inferior Italian troops waged a war against British forces for three long months. On 9 December the British, commanded by General Sir Archibald Wavell, launched a limited counteroffensive against Mussolini's army. Out in the baking-hot desert Italian forces fought a five-day battle of attrition that led to almost total disaster.

By early January 1941, the Italians had been pushed deep into Libya and were finally besieged by British and Commonwealth troops at Bardia. The exhausted and dispirited Italian troops fled for Tobruk, which finally fell to British forces on 21 January, yielding 27,000 prisoners. The remnants of Mussolini's forces retreated in disarray on Tripoli, the capital of Libya. It was here in Tripoli that the Italian dictator was compelled either to ask for help from Hitler, or face total annihilation. In fact, prior to the Italian invasion of Egypt, Hitler had actually offered Mussolini the assistance of a Panzer division, but the Italian dictator, more interested in a prestige victory, decided to decline a most reasonable offer. When Mussolini finally requested help Hitler readily accepted, for the Führer was determined to restore the Axis and consolidate the Reich's strategic position in North Africa.

For the defeat of the British in North Africa Hitler decided to use one charismatic leader who would stamp his greatest achievements in the desert. His name was General Erwin Rommel, the great Panzer leader who had led his 7.Panzer-Division through France in 1940 to victory.

By 14 February 1941, Rommel had arrived for the first time in Tripoli. He was ordered to command what was now named the *Deutsche Afrika-Korps*. This new armoured corps had only two Panzer divisions. The second Panzer division did not arrive until May 1941. The first unit was a light division, titled the 5.Light-Division. This division fielded some 150 tanks and nearly half of them were Pz.Kpfw.III and Pz.Kpfw.IV's. In addition the *Afrika-Korps* possessed a few 8.8cm anti-aircraft guns, which proved to be a very feared anti-tank weapon. Rommel used his '88's' to full effect against the British. When the allied tanks charged towards his Panzers,

Rommel ordered them to quickly withdraw behind their screen of 88mm guns, which, with greater range, would decimate advancing enemy armour. This technique was used in North Africa repeatedly and it was something the British were unable to counter.

Out in the desert Rommel stuck to the Blitzkrieg tactics of keeping his Panzers concentrated and employing them to achieve massive local superiority. By early March Rommel's *Afrika-Korps* were in action and were pushing back the British through the desert. In the first week of April, trying to keep their forces together, the British withdrew in panic from the peninsula of Cyrenaica. Rommel, on their tail, did not give them any freedom of withdrawal and instructed a dramatic three pronged all out assault, determined to exploit the enemy's confusion. As the enemy continued to withdraw, Rommel now believed that the port of Tobruk was in his grasp. Tobruk was the most important port in North Africa and since it was occupied by the British, the *Afrika-Korps* could not resume its offensive to Egypt until it was captured. But the garrison there was very strong, and held by the British Empire's toughest troops. Repeated attacks against Tobruk failed miserably. The 15.Panzer-Division was rushed to North Africa to help break the resistance, but still the enemy heroically held out. Rommel was compelled to bypass Tobruk and boldly push his forces further east.

Late in the summer of 1941, the *Afrika-Korps* was strengthened, upgraded and renamed *Panzergruppe Afrika* (Panzer Group Africa). It consisted of six Italian divisions, and included the *Afrika-Korps* – the 15. and 21.Panzer-Divisions – and the 90.Light-Division, which included old units from the 5.Light-Division. During this period the British did not waste any time and took the opportunity to reinforce their army, and had also reorganized the Western Desert Force as the British 8th Army under the command of Field-Marshal Montgomery.

By November the British were ready once again to do battle with Rommel. What began was a fierce tank battle across an area of about 130km from the Egyptian border in the east to Tobruk in the west. Rommel once again displayed mastery of mobile operations. But in late November the British lines stiffened and Rommel, exhausted and overstretched with no fuel ordered a general retreat from Cyrenaica. On Christmas day Benghazi fell into British hands, and by the end of the year the *Afrika-Korps* was back where it had first started.

During the first weeks of 1942 Rommel planned to retake what he had previously lost. On 21 January he unleashed his Panzer divisions across the desert and amazingly outwitted, outmanoeuvred and outgunned his bewildered enemy. By May *Panzergruppe Afrika* with more than 10,000 vehicles pushed through the desert. The leading spearheads of the drive reached Tobruk by mid-June. With massed aerial support and hundreds of pieces of artillery the port was pounded mercilessly into submission. By 21 June Tobruk finally fell. With its capture the British fled across the desert towards Egypt. Victory for Rommel was beckoning.

The Panzer divisions of the *Afrika-Korps* were now only 62km from the great British naval base at Alexandria. In Cairo, a state of emergency had been declared. Rommel's armoured drive continued to tear through the desert, bearing down on the Egyptian frontier. It advanced in broad formation against the well-fortified town of El Alamein, the last great obstacle before final victory. But after almost eighteen months of battling across the desert, the Panzer divisions were worn from constant combat. For the battle at El Alamein Rommel could only field some 207 Panzers against 767 of Montgomery's tanks. In spite of the dire situation on 30 August he prepared his divisions to do battle.

All along the German front Rommel's Panzers crashed into action, moving eastward through minefields which were heavily defended by infantry equipped with anti-tank guns. The British had been expecting the attack for some time and their defensive positions were almost impregnable. The ferociousness of the attack brought many causalities and loss of equipment. Within one week the *Afrika-Korps* was fighting for survival. Rommel had affectively lost the battle at El Alamein.

By early November Rommel was in full retreat. There would be no more Blitzkrieg tactics for the '*desert Fox*'. Instead he had to reluctantly plan the withdrawal of his entire force before they were lost forever, annihilated in the desert wilderness of North Africa. The once great armoured might of the *Afrika-Korps* was no more. It now consisted of shattered elements of 15, 21-Panzer-Division's, 5.Panzer-Regiment, 90.Light-African-Division and the *605.Panzerjager-Abteilung*. Even the new formidable Pz.Kpfw.IV '*Tiger*' tanks, which had been rushed to Tunisia to oppose allied armour, not enough to offset the German disadvantage.

By the end of April 1943 the lack of supplies was in so short supply that tank crews desperately tried to distil fuel for their remaining tanks from locally produced wines and spirits. But still this did not avert defeat, it just prolonged the agony.

On 13 May with no more territory remaining to defend, the last elements of the German and Italian forces in North Africa passed into allied captivity.

An Sd.Kfz.7/1 halftrack is unloaded at the port of Tripoli following the first despatch of German troops, guns, and armoured vehicles to North Africa, which took place on 14 February 1941. The first units to arrive were comprised of the advanced echelon troops of the 5.Light and 3.Panzer-Regiments, as well as reconnaissance soldiers and support units.

An interesting photograph showing a Pz.Kpfw.IV Ausf.D out in the middle of the desert. The crew have utilised the frame of a soft skinned truck for a makeshift shelter. Perched on the turret roof is an Sfl4Z scissors field periscope. The periscope was able to estimate ranges, but provided a rather narrow range.

Two Pz.Kpfw.III`s supported by a number of light Horch cross-country vehicles advance along a sandy road bound for the front lines. Out in the desert the Germans used their Blitzkrieg tactics and deployed armour, motorised infantry and airpower in coordinated attacks for rapid penetrations.

General Erwin Rommel, the great Panzer commander of the new Deutsche Afrika-Korps, confers with his staff during operations in the western desert. Rommel had absolute conviction in mobile operations and believed in leading his Panzer force from the front.

A group of soldiers standing next to the field kitchen trailer, clearly showing the special aluminium food containers. A field kitchen was a very important component to any infantry or Panzer division on the battlefield. Where possible the Germans went to great lengths supplying their men with rations of warm food.

Another photograph showing the same group of soldiers standing next to a trailer carrying what appears to be a field kitchen utensil containing soup or similar food. A motorcycle combination can be seen camouflaged in the familiar sand base colour of the Deutsche Afrika-Korps.

German officers demonstrate to their Italian allies the use of artillery in the desert. In a Panzer division there were usually three fully mechanized batteries in an artillery regiment: two field batteries of 12 10.5cm gun howitzers, and one medium battery with one troop of four 10.5cm guns and four 15cm gun howitzers.

An eight-wheeled Sd.Kfz.231 heavy armoured car during operations in July 1941. These vehicles were unique among German armoured cars in the Panzer divisions. All eight wheels were individually powered, which ensured that the vehicle could still move even after enemy fire damaged one or more of its wheels.

In the desert are two light Horch cross-country vehicles, a Volkswagen Type 82 166 Kfz.1 light personnel carrier, and a specially adapted Opel Blitz truck fitted with a 2cm Flak 30 light anti-aircraft gun. Throughout the North African campaign the Germans constantly improvised and utilised a number of commercial vehicles to carry anti-aircraft guns.

From his staff car the 'Desert Fox' confers with his officers. Rommel's vehicle distinctively carries the divisional emblem of the *Deutsches Afrika Korps*, which was a white palm tree with a swastika. The vehicle also displays a white tactical sign, and on the mudguard a command formation sign indicating that it belongs to the 'Corps Headquarters'.

Vehicles spread out across the vast desert as far as the eye can see. These vehicles belong to rear units of the 15.Panzer-Division during its rapid drive through the western desert in September 1941. Already the Panzer division was becoming overstretched and exhausted.

Two Pz.Kpfw.III's have halted in the desert. These tanks belong to the 15.Panzer-Division. The division had arrived in North Africa in April 1941. Within seven months the division had been reduced to a handful of operational tanks and had to be withdrawn for refitting. However, early the following year it received additional vehicles when it took part in the Battle of El Alamein.

In front of a light personnel carrier laden with supplies on the roof, a group of officers attached to an unidentified regiment of the 15.Panzer-Division have stopped in the middle of the desert to confer about the general situation. They are all wearing the greatcoat and the best-known item of tropical field dress, the peaked field cap, or Afrika Korps Feldmütze.

In action against enemy armour in early 1942 is a flak crew firing their deadly 8.8cm flak gun. Because of their speed and mobility across open desert, a flak detachment was a very formidable unit. In the distance plumes of black smoke rise up into the air, suggesting a number of enemy vehicles have been hit and destroyed.

A Pz.Kpfw.III advances across the desert supported by infantry on foot. A variety of other armoured vehicles can be seen in the distance. When advancing in open desert like this, tank crews were often taught to use the famous Afrika-Korps `V` formation. A battalion of about 75 tanks used this formation, with two companies leading and one in reserve.

An Sdk.Kfz.251 Ausf.B of the divisional staff races through the desert. The halftrack is equipped with a good long-range radio set with a large tubular antenna. The divisional staff used the vehicle as the lifeblood to travel to various parts of the front. At any chosen point they were able to be contacted or issue orders to the divisional headquarters or various commands.

A photograph taken from a light cross-country vehicle shows Pz.Kpfw.IIIs moving across the desert in their familiar V-formation. The tanks are heavily laden with supplies, which can be seen stowed on the engine deck.

A knocked out Pz.Kpfw.IV in the desert in early 1943. This is just one of many hundreds of destroyed and abandoned vehicles of the once vaunted Afrika-Korps. The Pz.Kpfw. had been used as the main striking force in the Panzer divisions against the British.

Chapter Seven

Battles on the Eastern Front

By the end of 1941 the battle weary Panzer divisions, which had taken part in Operation Barbarossa, were no longer fit to fight. Mobile operations had consequently ground to a halt. Fortunately for the exhausted Panzer crews and supporting units no mobile operations had been planned during the winter of 1941, let alone for 1942. In the freezing arctic temperatures the majority of the Panzer divisions were pulled out of their stagnant defensive positions and transferred to France, to rest, reorganize and retrain.

In spite of the terrible problems that faced the badly depleted Panzer divisions, back in Germany production of tanks still increased. In order to overcome the mammoth task of defeating the Red Army, more Panzer divisions were being raised and motorised divisions converted into panzergrenadier divisions. Although equipping the Panzer divisions was a slow and expensive process, it was undertaken effectively with the introduction of a number of new fresh divisions being deployed on the front lines.

However, by the beginning of the summer offensive in May 1942, not all the Panzer divisions were fully equipped and ready for combat. Some of the older units for instance did not even have their losses from the winter offensive of 1941 replaced and were not ready for any type of full-scale operation. Worn out and depleted Panzer divisions were therefore relegated to Army Group North or Army Group Centre where they were hastily deployed for a series of defensive actions instead. The best-equipped Panzer divisions were shifted south to Army Group South for operations through the Caucasus. This was entrusted to the two Panzer Armies – 1st and 4th – that were to spearhead the drive. By May 1942 most of the Panzer divisions involved were up to nearly eighty five percent of their original fighting strength, and been equipped with Pz.Kpfw.III's and Pz.Kpfw.IV's. Three additional brand new Panzer divisions, numbers 22, 23, and 24 were quickly deployed for action in the Panzer Armies. The divisions had a combined strength of 495 tanks, 181 of which were concentrated in the 24.Panzer-Division. Although these Panzer divisions were the best equipped for operations in the East and almost to strength, the 22.Panzer-Division however, was in terrible short supply of tanks and bolstered by 114 obsolete and undergunned Pz.Kpfw.38 (t).

Although the great, rivers Donetz, Don, Volga and Terek, were seen by Panzer commanders as great obstacles, the Caucasus area was ideal tank country and the Panzer divisions were expected to carve their way through Red Army positions just as they had done the previous summer. It seemed that there was renewed confidence and the Panzer war of 1942 appeared to be on the verge of victory. The summer offensive was scheduled to begin in earnest on 28 June. Some 15 Panzer divisions and Panzergrenadier divisions of the 1st and 4th Armies, together with Italian, Rumanian and Hungarian formations crashed into action. In just two days the leading spearheads had pushed 150km deep into the enemy lines and began to cut off the city of Voronezh. The city fell on 7 July. The two Panzer armies then converged with all their might on Stalingrad. It seemed that the Russians were now doomed. With an air of confidence Hitler decided to abandon the armoured advance on Stalingrad and embark on an encirclement operation down on the Don. The 6th Army was to go on and capture Stalingrad without any real Panzer support and fight a bloody battle of attrition there. Eventually the fighting became so fierce it embroiled some 21 German divisions including six Panzer and Panzergrenadier divisions.

The 6th Army soon became encircled and three hurriedly reorganised understrength Panzer divisions were thrown into a relief operation. By 19 December the 6.Panzer-Division had fought its way to within 50km of Stalingrad. But under increasing Russian pressure the relief operation failed. The 6.Panzer-Division and remnants of the 4th Panzer Army were forced to retreat, leaving the 6th Army in the encircled city to its fate. Some 94,000 soldiers surrendered on 2 February 1943. With them the 14, 16, and 24.Panzer-Divisions, and the 3, 29, and 60.Panzergrenadier-Divisions were decimated.

The end now seemed destined to unfold, but still more resources were poured into the Panzer divisions. Throughout the early cold months of 1943, the *Panzerwaffe* built up strength of the badly depleted Panzer divisions. By the summer they fielded some 24 Panzer divisions on the Eastern Front alone. This was a staggering transformation of a Panzer force that had lost immeasurable amounts of armour in less than two years of combat. Hitler now intended to risk his precious Panzer divisions in what became the largest tank battle of World War Two, Operation *Zitadelle*.

In June 1943, 21 Panzer divisions, including four *Waffen-SS* divisions and two Panzergrenadier divisions were being prepared for Operation *Zitadelle* in the Kursk salient. For this massive attack the *Panzerwaffe* were able to muster in early July 17 divisions and two brigades with no less than 1,715 Panzers and 147 *Sturmegeschutz* III (StuG) assault guns. Each division averaged some 98 Panzers and self-propelled anti-tank guns. The new Pz.Kpfw.V 'Panther' Ausf.A made its debut, despite its production problems.

Putting together such a strong force was a great achievement, but the Panzer divisions of 1943 were unlike those armoured forces that had victoriously steamrolled across western Russia two years earlier. In fact, to make matters worse, by the time the final date had been set for the attack as the 4 July, the Red Army knew the German plans and they had made their preparations. It was therefore not surprising that the Panzer divisions were unable to break through the strong Soviet defences. The new *Panther* too even failed to meet the expectations on the battlefield and was constantly hindered by mechanical problems. This first *Panther* model actually earned the nickname *'Guderian's problem child'*. Around two hundred of these tanks were sent to the Kursk area, and most broke down. The Pz.Kpfw.VI. *'Tiger'* too experienced problems, especially with the retrieval of vehicles, which were damaged by the extensive Russian minefields.

As for the other tanks and armoured vehicles they also succumbed to what became known as the disaster at Kursk. Skilful Russian anti-tank fire brought many of the vehicles to a flaming halt, in spite a number of successful breakthroughs across minefields and anti-tank obstacles. The 4th Panzer Army had managed a 35km advance before it too was abruptly halted. A week into the attack the 9th Army was compelled to break off the attack to fight off a massive Red Army counter attack from its rear at Orel.

On 13 July Hitler wasted no time and ordered all operations round Kursk to be called off before all his forces were totally decimated. The losses at Kursk were immense. The Panzer divisions had suffered irreparable losses – including 3,000 Panzers and 5,000 other vehicles. The loss had marked the end of the massed German Panzer assaults in the East forever. The Panzer and infantry divisions now took the first steps of their slow painful retreat back to Germany. The Red Army had managed to destroy no less than 30 divisions, seven of which were Panzer. Now exhausted and half ruined, the Panzer divisions were insufficient to replace the staggering losses. They fought on in desperation under strength.

At the start of August, the Red Army continued its drive, pushing back the *Panzerwaffe*. Within a matter of weeks it had quickly gained all its lost ground round Kursk. By the end of the month Kharkov was retaken. What followed in the ensuing weeks and months to come was a general German retreat with the Russians repossessing lost territory.

Prime movers towing heavy artillery in a snow blizzard following Army Group Centre's failure to capture Moscow. In front of the Russian capital hundreds of tanks had been abandoned in the drifting snow, and the crews retreated on foot. In four Panzer divisions alone there were just a handful of tanks that were able to operate effectively.

A Pz.Kpfw.IV and Pz.Kpfw.III Ausf.J pass a Volkswagen Type 82 166 Kfz.1 cross-country light personnel carrier. The Pz.Kpfw.III appears to have received an application of white wash paint in order to help camouflage the vehicle against the snow.

A Pz.Kpfw.III Ausf.J halted in the snow during operations in early 1942. This particular variant mounted a very powerful long-barrelled 5cm (1.97in) KwK 39 L/60 gun. In total there were some 2516 Ausf.J variants that were built between March 1941 and July 1942.

A Pz.Kpfw.III parked at the roadside in a Russian village during operations in January 1942. The first Russian winter had ground the Panzer divisions to a halt. Instead of attacking in their familiar Blitzkrieg style they were compelled to desperately defend their flanks by units that had become isolated in the snow with hardly any useable vehicles.

A Pz.Kpfw.III moves along a road during the early spring of 1942. The vehicle has two sets of track links bolted to the front of its hull for additional armoured protection. As with many vehicles of this period the Panzers were still painted in overall dark grey.

A long column of Pz.Kpfw.III`s during fresh operations in May 1942. The best-equipped Panzer divisions were shifted south for the long drive through the Caucasus. These Panzers belong to the new 24.Panzer-Division, which had been equipped with mainly Pz.Kpfw.III`s and IV`s.

A Wehrmacht Luftwaffe flak detachment is preparing their 8.8cm flak gun for action. As heavier more lethal Soviet armour was brought to bear against the Germans in 1942, the Panzer divisions increased their anti-aircraft battalions, each of which contained two or even three heavy batteries.

A Pz.Kpfw.III moves along a road churning up dust. Note the rolled-up canvas sheeting on the rear of the engine deck which, when pulled over the top of the vehicle and tied down, formed a kind of canopy and broke up outlines of the tank. The canopy was primarily used to protect the crew from aerial attack by disguising it.

A flak crew on standby with their 8.8cm flak gun. In some sectors of the Eastern Front, several units had barely enough Panzers to oppose the Russian armour and called upon flak battalions to help break the Red Army's relentless determination to hold to the bitter end.

A number of Pz.Kpfw.IV`s being transported by rail to another area of operations on the Eastern Front. The main factor in the success of the Panzer divisions in Russia was their speed and mobility and the ability to be quickly and effectively transported by rail. Often, when a Panzer division was withdrawn from the front, the Russians would claim it had been destroyed, only to find it would reappear a few days later several hundred kilometres away.

Pz.Kpfw.III`s and IV's during the winter battles of late 1942. All of the Panzers have received a very crude coating of winter white wash paint. Once the snow had disappeared crews were able to easily wash off the paint to reveal its original camouflage colours.

The crew of a StuG.III Ausf.F pose for the camera during the early spring of 1943. This powerful assault gun went into production in mid-1942. It mounted a longer 7.5cm StuK 40 L/43 gun and saw extensive action on the Eastern Front.

A stationary Pz.Kpfw.VI Tiger.I on the Eastern Front in 1943. This is probably the most famous of the Panzers that saw action in the Panzer divisions. It was primarily built in response to the heavy and powerful Soviet tanks like the KV I and II and the T-34.

A heavily camouflaged StuG.III Ausf.G halted on a road in central Russia in the spring of 1943. By this period the StuG.III had become a very common assault gun in the Panzer divisions, with some 3041 one of them becoming operational in that year alone. This particular variant was armed with a 7.5cm StuK 40 L/48 gun and also carried for local defence a 7.92mm MG34 machine gun.

A line of Pz.Kpfw.IV`s off the production line and preparing to be shipped out to the Eastern Front to help bolster the Panzer divisions. This new variant dominated the Panzer divisions in which it served. Its firepower was more than capable of knocking out the Soviet T-34.

A new Pz.Kpfw.IV has just been delivered to a regiment in Russia in the spring of 1943. The vehicle has not yet received any type of camouflage paint scheme for the local terrain. It was sometimes left to the maintenance teams or even the crews themselves to paint the vehicle with a camouflage pattern.

A Pz.Kpfw.IV Ausf.G is being reloaded with shells, which can be seen being passed through the side turret hatch by a crewman. The vehicle is painted with a camouflage scheme of light green spots over the dark sand base.

Almost a full company of StuG.III Ausf.F's parked on a forest road. These had been up-armoured and re-armed with a longer-barrelled 7.5cm gun giving them a genuine anti-tank capability. Throughout 1943 the StuG.III demonstrated its mettle in the Panzer divisions and was a sought after machine with the Panzergrenadiers.

A StuG.III Ausf.F during operations in Russia in the spring of 1943. Note the kill rings painted in white on the 7.5cm barrel. This was wide spread practice in the German military units to paint victory or kill ring markings on guns or vehicles that had destroyed enemy vehicles, aircraft or other targets.

StuG.III wades across a river with Panzergrenadiers clinging to the vehicle. On the opposite side of the riverbank it is evident by the sight of destroyed buildings that heavy artillery has played a key part before the armoured strike was implemented.

A Pz.Kpfw.IV halts during its advance and traverses it turret, aiming its deadly 7.5cm barrel, making sure the enemy target has been annihilated. Behind the tank black oily smoke obscures the area suggesting that enemy vehicles have been destroyed. There appears to be little chance of conflict now as two officers can be seen standing talking to the crew.

A Pz.Bef.Wg.III command tank crossing a pontoon bridge during operations in the early summer of 1943. Note the prominent rod antenna mounted on the left side and the frame antenna seen fitted on the engine deck. Inside the frame antenna is a stowage bin.

A number of armoured vehicles have halted inside a devastated captured town. The crew of a Pz.Kpfw.III take a much-needed respite and relax on the turret. Note the other Pz.Kpfw.III laden with supplies. Fitted to the rear of the engine deck is a fuel drum. The long distances in which these vehicles had to travel were a constant problem for re-supply.

Panzer crews training with two Pz.Kpfw.IV`s in Western Russia in mid-1943. Because these vehicles were technically advanced and complex machines a special training manual was produced. Particular emphasis was drawn on combat experience on the Eastern Front and it laid down 30 rules primarily aimed at junior officer level.

Rolling forward across the vast expanse of the Soviet Union are Sd.Kfz.8 halftrack prime movers towing sFH18 heavy field howitzers. By this period of the war the Soviet Air Force increasingly dominated the sky. Armoured crews therefore went to great lengths camouflaging their vehicles and heavy weapons with foliage.

A Pz.Kpfw.IV passing through a Russian village. Note the puppy on the wireless operator's hatch. Throughout the first half of 1943 a great number of Pz.Kpfw.IV`s entered service for action in the East. Slowly the *Panzerwaffe* built up its strength, and by the summer of 1943 they fielded some 24 Panzer divisions in Russia alone.

A variety of vehicles from the 20.Panzer-Division move forward during the initial stages of the armoured offensive at Kursk on 5 July 1943. With its 120 Panzer and assault guns the division broke through Red Army lines of defence and succeeded in advancing 5km with the help of intense artillery support.

Late version Pz.Kpfw.IV`s open fire on Red Army targets during the Kursk offensive, code-named Zitadelle. Note the side skirts or schürzen. The vehicle's protective skirts were made of mild steel plates and were designed to protect the tank from rounds fired at close range by Russian anti-tank fire.

During Zitadelle a Wespe self-propelled artillery gun belonging to an armoured regiment of the Grossdeutschland Division moves into position camouflaged by undergrowth. The vehicle was armed with a potent 10.5cm leFH 18/2 L/28 gun and was relatively successful during the battles fought around Kursk.

Undertaking repairs to a Pz.Kpfw.IV in 1943. Much was owed to these maintenance companies, which kept the vehicles in fighting condition. The Panzer is covered with Zimmerit, an anti-magnetic mine coating which began to be applied in the factory to virtually all German tanks and assault guns by September 1943.

The most famous vehicles to appear at Zitadelle were the Pz.Kpfw.V Panther and Pz.Kpfw.VI Tiger I. Here in this photograph is a column of Tigers moving along a dirt road with troops hitching a lift. The Tiger played a prominent role in Russia, and was used with lethal effect at Kursk.

A Pz.Kpfw.V Panther Ausf.D in the summer of 1943. One of the crew poses for the camera sprawled out across the vehicle's gun cleaning tube. The Panther still retains its old smoke candle dischargers that were fitted on either side of the turret. This practice ceased in June 1943 after a reported incident earlier that year, when enemy small arms had set off the dischargers, incapacitating the crew.

Late 1943 and a Pz.Kpfw.IV with an application of winter white wash paint moves through a village. Note the protective covering on the 7.5cm gun barrel's muzzle brake and the MG 34 machine gun. The use of protective covering was quite common practice, especially to avoid dust and mud entering the barrel.

Tiger tanks retreating during the winter of late 1943. All the vehicles have received winter white wash paint, and even the Panzer crews are wearing white reversible camouflage smocks. Note the Panzergrenadiers hitching a lift on board the tank.

Chapter Eight

Defeat in the West

The Germans were fully aware of the allied invasion of northern France, but predicting where it was due to take place was difficult to ascertain. Along the so-called impregnable West-wall, running from Norway to the Mediterranean, stood 10 Panzer, 17 infantry and 31 training or coastal defence divisions. On paper it seemed impressive, but in reality many of the formations were poor quality and understrength. On the Eastern Front the Germans had suffered over two million casualties alone and replacements to fill these dwindling ranks could only be achieved with the young and old. Battlefield losses to vehicles were also immense and as the war continued through the dark days of 1944, each surviving tank became an asset. War-ravaged German factories also could no longer keep pace with the increasing demand of vehicles for the Panzer divisions to match those already destroyed. In a desperate attempt to avert the inevitable disaster, Hitler placed high priority on the production of new tanks over the supply of vital replacement parts and engines. But the Eastern Front was bleeding the Panzer divisions dry of vehicles. Another problem that faced the Panzerwaffe in the East was that vital armour was being transferred to the west to meet the possible threat of a second front. Several Panzer divisions were moved to France to meet the threat. Among them were some new Panzer divisions established in 1943 and early 1944.

In early June 1944, the Germans had a total of nine Panzer divisions in France with 1,673 tanks and assault guns. Among them were the Panzer-Lehr-Division, 116.Panzer-Division and the 12.SS.Panzer-Division 'Hitlerjugend'. Although most of these Panzer divisions were curtailed by shortages, they still enjoyed superiority in the quality of their tanks' forces. Not only were crews generally very experienced due to years of fighting on the Eastern Front, but the tanks they used were far better than those used by the allies. In particular were the Panther, Tiger and new King Tiger tanks, which had complete superiority on the battlefield. However, because they were manufactured in such short numbers it was to have a very real impact on the coming battles ahead in France.

When the allies finally unleashed the largest amphibious landing in military history upon the shores of the Normandy beaches on 6 June, the only German armoured formation to be engaged against the allies was the 21.Panzer-Division. It was commanded by Field-Marshal Erwin Rommel. The division's main battle tank was the Pz.Kpfw.IV, but it was also forced to use captured French tanks from 1940. Although bolstered with antiquated armour, nonetheless, the 21.Panzer-Division did have some success and managed to break through superior allied lines.

By the middle of June the allies were still making slow costly progress through the Normandy blockage. Hitler released more Panzer divisions and soon the British found they were opposed by no less than six Panzer divisions in and around the city of Caen. But it was too late, Caen fell and this led to the allied breakout.

As the American offensive gathered momentum, the British forces took advantage of confused German units to form a northern pincer of a huge encircling movement, designed solely to trap German units in Normandy in a huge pocket centred on the town of Falaise. By 20 August the British had linked up the drive southwards with American forces to close a ring around Falaise. What took place inside the pocket was catastrophic for the German divisions trapped inside. Death, carnage and devastation littered the Falaise pocket as German units tried in vain to escape the slaughter. Almost 60,00 troops were trapped inside along with almost the entire armoured compliment defending the Western Front. Although 40,000 German troops managed to escape, some 10,000 Germans died. By the end of August the allies had destroyed the Panzer divisions concentrated in the west. Reported German strength of all the remaining units amounted to just 70 tanks and assault guns out of 1,600 that were deployed in France. Most trucks, guns and equipment were lost. The remaining armoured vehicles withdrew across the Meuse River during the relative safety of the night, fearing if they travelled by day they would be certainly destroyed altogether by aerial attack.

After the destruction at Falaise all the reserves had gone. They had either been put into battle and lost, or were trying to helplessly fill the dwindling ranks. The Panzer divisions were now a shadow of their former self. In late August, in a desperate move to strengthen its forces, independent Panzer brigades were rushed into service. The majority were hastily absorbed into the various Panzer divisions, which needed to have their badly depleted ranks quickly replenished. However, the bulk of the Panzer divisions were loosely organized ad hoc groups. Their armament was mixed and more often undergunned, and because they had no time to train and refit properly, they were regularly sent to the front to help prop-up the disintegrating lines with severe consequences. With insufficient fuel and insufficient or incorrect ammunition supplies the remaining Panzer divisions reluctantly withdrew from France.

The high rate of attrition on the armoured force caused the German tank designers to find a desperate solution. Instead of producing brand new tanks, which would take many man hours to manufacture, the Germans utilised the excellent chassis's of the Pz.Kpfw.IV's, Tiger's and Panther's to produce a machine that would perhaps slow the allied advance. The tanks were converted into the Jagdpanzer IV, Jagdpanther and Jagdtiger. These new tank killers with heavier firepower than ever before were perfectly suited for defensive battles. However, by December 1944, these new variants were to be used for an offensive role, that not even the allies dreamed would be possible in the final months of the war.

In November Hitler planned a bold counter-offensive in the West. He chose the hilly and wooded terrain of the Ardennes, scene of his 1940 campaign. The striking power comprised of the 5th and 6th Panzer Armies to which had been given the bulk of the Panzers that could be scraped together. The aim of the offensive was to break through towards Antwerp, drive a wedge between the British and Americans, isolate the British force, cut its supply lines and then crush it before turning on the Americans.

The offensive, code-named 'Wacht Am Rhein' or 'Watch on the Rhine', began in earnest on the morning of 16 December. Remarkably the Germans had pulled together almost 1,000 tanks, 2,000 artillery pieces and 250,000 soldiers for the attack. This was an exceptional feat of planning, and when the force actually crashed into action it totally surprised the allies. The 5th Panzer Army bulldozed it's way through American lines and in the first day advance Panzer units had crossed over the river Our. The powerful 6th Panzer Army, also consisting of well-seasoned Waffen-SS Panzer divisions, made good progress causing severe losses to allied forces. For a few days the German plan seemed to be going well. But four miles short of the Meuse the offensive was slowed and stopped. Fuel shortages and the lack of other supplies coupled with the winter weather and ever-growing allied air pressure made the end inevitable. As for the new tank killers, the devastating combination of artillery fire and mastery of the skies meant there were few hiding places for these huge cumbersome machines.

By the end of January 1945 the front line was back to where it had been at the start of the German offensive six weeks earlier. The remnants of the 6th Panzer Army were sent to Russia, where a new Red Army offensive had burst along the Eastern Front. The men of the 6th Army left behind 100,000 men in the West either killed, wounded or captured, plus 800 tanks destroyed. As for the remaining Panzer divisions in the West, Hitler had nothing left at his disposal to counter the threat to the 'homeland'. His last gamble in the West had completely failed and the end of the Third Reich was in sight.

Grenadiers of the 12.SS Panzer-Division *Hitlerjugend* advance towards the city of Caen supported by Pz.Kpfw.IV`s. Under the command of SS-Standartenführer Kurt 'Panzer' Meyer, a battle group of three battalions of infantry and armour from the division's Panzer regiment along with the 21.Panzer-Division, temporarily stopped the allied assault.

The crewmembers pose for the camera onboard their StuG.III. Ausf.G during the Normandy campaign in 1944. Note the lack of foliage over the vehicle, which made it more susceptible to attack. The destruction of the Panzer divisions in France resulted from overwhelming enemy air power.

Two crewmembers pose for the camera in front of their well-camouflaged *Jagdpanzer* 38(t) *Hetzer* Tank Destroyer. The Hetzer was an effective tank-hunting machine. It was armed with a 7.5cm PaK 39 cannon and was used in France alongside the Panzer divisions to hunt and attack formations of much larger allied tanks.

A 7.5cm Pak 40 heavy anti-tank gun during intensive action in northern France in July 1944. In service it proved a powerful and deadly weapon, especially in the hands of well-trained anti-tank gunners. The Pak 40 became the most prolific German anti-tank weapon of the war.

On the Western front is a well dug-in and camouflaged Jagdpanzer 38(t) Hetzer. The vehicle was a very cheap, fuel-efficient tank destroyer and was widely used on the Western Front until the end of the war. Like the StuG these vehicles only equipped Panzer and Panzergrenadier divisions in exceptional cases.

A Pz.Kpfw.V `Panther` Ausf.D being prepared to be transported from the Italian front to northern France during the summer of 1944. The vehicle still retains its sand base camouflage colour scheme for the Italian campaign, and has no application of Zimmerit anti magnetic mine paste.

A Pz.Kpfw.V `Panther` Ausf.D parked at the roadside. This vehicle was undoubtedly an excellent battle tank. It combined a formidable mix of firepower, armour and mobility, outclassing most of its opponents such as the T34/76 and Sherman.

A StuG.III crew pose for the camera. In Normandy the StuG, although in considerably lower numbers than in the East, fought well. Due to their low bodies they were less vulnerable to enemy fire. However, they were more susceptible in close combat and less independent in combat with allied infantry.

A number of `Panther's` are beginning their journey by rail from the `homeland` bound for the Western front in the summer of 1944. In total there were some 409 `Panther's` that were deployed for action in the West. Altogether the *Panzerwaffe* had scraped-up 1513 armoured vehicles and distributed them between nine Panzer divisions and one Panzergrenadier division.

A knocked out Jagdpanzer IV/70 Tank Destroyer. This vehicle was well liked among its crews and became a very effective tank destroyer in the last year of the war. However, due to the large and heavy 7.5cm PaK 39 barrel, it helped ruin cross-country handling and slow down the overall effectiveness whilst it was in battle.

A StuG.III Ausf.G advances along a road. The vehicle appears have been embroiled in some fighting due to the missing schürzen plates. The StuG.III undoubtedly bolstered the dwindling armour in the Panzer divisions and provided sterling offensive service during the later stages of the war.

American troops examine a knocked out StuG.III.Ausf.G during the battle of France in the summer of 1944. A dead StuG crewman can be seen hanging over the 7.5cm gun barrel. It is more than likely that the corpse was purposely placed there for this photograph.

A StuG.III Ausf.G during operations in Normandy in the summer of 1944. Foliage has been attached to the vehicle in order to try and break up the StuG's distinctive shape, and thus minimise the possibility of aerial attack. By this period of the war the Panzer divisions were suffering terrible losses in northern France due to Allied air supremacy.

A StuG.III Ausf.G wades across a river laden with Panzergrenadiers hitching a lift. Note the horseshoe attached to the rear of the vehicle in order to give the superstitious crew good luck. A coating of Zimmerit anti-magnetic mine paste can evidently be seen sprayed over the entire vehicle.

French women and children with the few belongings they have left pass a knocked out Wespe self -propelled artillery gun. The vehicle has still foliage attached to the chassis and 10.5cm gun barrel. The Panzer divisions in France suffered massive losses from aerial bombardments and this led to the almost total destruction of the *Panzerwaffe* in the summer of 1944.

A StuG.III Ausf.G advances along a road in northern France accompanied by motorcyclists and another armoured vehicle. Foliage can clearly be seen strewn over the engine deck and tank tracks have been fitted to the hull for additional armoured protection.

Panzergrenadiers hitch a ride onboard a StuG.III Ausf.G during heavy fighting in the Normandy sector in July 1944. The vehicle still has a protective sleeve over the muzzle break of the barrel. The camouflage scheme over the intact Schürzen is green and brown wavy lines applied over the dark sand base.

A group of StuG.III Ausf.G`s roll along a French road supported by Panzergrenadiers on foot. Of the 248 assault guns reported in the West in June 1944, the majority were lost. A great number of them were destroyed as a result of vigorous allied fighter-bomber attacks.

A Pz.Kpfw.IV passes a stationary Pz.Kpfw.VI.Tiger.I. Both vehicles have plenty of foliage attached to the turret in order to minimise the high possibility of attack during the daylight hours. Note the attachment of spare road wheels to the rear of the Pz.Kpfw.IV for additional armoured protection.

Shells being loaded into a StuG.IV by an ammunition troop during combat in northern France. Although well armed, losses of equipment in the assault gun units had increased markedly in the course of the retreat through France. Often the vehicles were abandoned with minor damage and could not be towed away for lack of towing vehicles.

A Pz.Kpfw.V `Panther` Ausf.D with the preparation of Zimmerit anti-magnetic mine paste which can clearly be seen visible over the entire chassis. Although the Panther dominated the battlefields of the latter half of the war, they were never available in sufficient numbers to alter the course of the battle.

A well camouflaged StuG.III Ausf.G inside a destroyed French town. By 1944 the assault guns were a very popular vehicle supporting the slowly diminishing Panzer divisions. But the fortunes of war in 1944 forced the StuG onto the Strategic defensive. Growing shortages of tanks meant that the assault guns were being rapidly used in areas of the front incompatible with its design and training.

Tiger IV's from *SS.Pz.Abt.101* in Normandy. The Tiger saw extensive action in the Normandy sector and was a fearsome vehicle to the British and American tankers. Its thick frontal armour meant that the only allied tank with a chance of taking out a Tiger was the Sherman Firefly.

Sprawled out as far as the eye can see are a wide variety of vehicles and troops withdrawing through Holland in September 1944. The campaign in France had been costly to both the infantry and Panzer divisions, with many of its finest units all being destroyed. Following the comprehensive defeat in France, remnants of the Panzer divisions were withdrawn for rest and refitting.

The final battles in France and grenadiers supported by a StuG.III Ausf.G fight a bitter defence in a hastily dug trench. During the battles in France grenadiers relied heavily on fire support from the StuG.III, which was at its best fighting from defensive positions against advancing enemy armoured formations.

Withdrawing into Belgium in September 1944, a column of unidentified late variant armoured vehicles and infantry hastily try and salvage what is left of its destroyed units and move to the relative safety of the Low Countries to rest and refit. By this time, all reserves were gone; the Panzer divisions were now a mere shadow of their former self.

Preparing for the Ardennes offensive in November 1944. A company of StuG.III Ausf.G`s with supporting vehicles await for orders to move to their specially assigned jump-off areas along the Belgium and Luxembourg borders. Assault guns figured prominently among the Panzer divisions committed to the Ardennes operation. The vehicle's low silhouette and fuel economy made it an obvious choice in the wooded and hilly terrain.

A rare shot of a Tiger.I with an application of winter whitewash paint over a coating of Zimmerit during the early phase of the Ardennes operation in December 1944. By this time production of the Tiger I had been terminated in favour of the superior Tiger II or King Tiger.

A Hummel self-propelled gun being prepared to be transported by rail from Germany to the Ardennes in November 1944. These vehicles were incorporated into batteries of six Hummels and allocated to advance through the Ardennes in support of the main armoured drive.

A StuG.III Ausf.G advances through a Belgian village during the later stages of the Ardennes offensive in January 1945. Note the BMW motorcycle attached to the StuG`s offside rear. The stowage bins mounted on the engine deck can be seen left in an open position.

Chapter Nine

The End Comes

By January and February 1944 the Soviet offensives were grinding even further west with the Panzer divisions losing even more armour in the process. To make matters worse, the threat of an allied invasion in the West also compelled Hitler to draw off vital armoured units in Russia and shift them to northern France.

Four months later, on the morning of 22 June, the third anniversary of the Soviet invasion, a massive Russian offensive, code named Operation *Bagration*, was launched against Army Group Centre. The three German armies opposing them had thirty-seven divisions, weakly supported by armour, against 166 divisions, supported by 2,700 tanks and 1,300 assault guns. At the end of the first week of *Bagration* the three German armies had lost between them nearly 200,000 men and 900 tanks; 9th Army and the 3rd Panzer Army were almost decimated. The remnants of the shattered armies trudged back west in order to try and rest and refit what was left of its Panzer units and build new defensive lines. Any plans to regain the initiative on the Eastern Front were doomed forever. With the Red Army advancing at break-neck speed it was only a matter of time before it threatened Hungary, Rumania and Bulgaria.

During the summer of 1944 the *Panzerwaffe* sent a substantial quantity of armour to the Bulgarian Army in a drastic attempt to defend its frontier from the Russians. Precious Panzer divisions were also removed from Russia to Hungary where they were commanded to take part in Operation Spring Awakening to re-take Budapest in order to secure Germany's dwindling oil stocks. To move the Panzer divisions quickly and effectively to Hungary they had to be moved all the way across Europe by loading and transporting them by rail. The logistical problems in late 1944 were immense and it was a huge complex problem transporting them from the Western Front without risk of aerial attack. The Panzer divisions were almost defenceless against enemy fighter-bombers, which flew over continually, but fortunately for Sepp Dietrich's 6th SS Panzer Army they arrived in Hungary safely, and were soon preparing their forces for a doomed mission to capture the Hungarian capital.

Elsewhere on the Eastern Front, the German position offered little comfort to the

Panzer crews and supporting units that had to try and defend every yard of territory. By the winter of late 1944 German forces had retreated through Poland and were fighting the most titanic of conflicts with hardly anything left. Since early 1943 wide-ranging Panzer operations and the total reliance upon armour to carry out an offensive or to create defensive positions could no longer be relied on to support infantry. Instead, soldiers fought and defended without any real armoured support. Consequently the losses were immense.

In the West the military situation was just as grim. After the crushing defeat of the Ardennes offensive, the remaining Panzer divisions in the West were pulled back to construct new defenses along the borders of Germany. Despite the deteriorating situation in the West a number of Panzers and support units were again pulled out of the ranks to fill up the diminishing strength of those forces desperately fighting for survival on the Eastern Front.

Although the weight in Panzer numbers was now running out on both the Western and Eastern Fronts, the diminishing units of the Panzer divisions managed incredible feats of action and staying power. Even after the Ardennes offensive in the West there followed another strategic offensive code-named 'Nordwind'. This limited operation was intended to recapture Strasbourg, but failed. Thereafter, German armoured operations were conducted in local, tactical attacks against western allied forces pushing eastward through the Siegfried Line, across the Rhine and deep into the *Reich*.

In Russia the tactical situation was similar, but fighting conditions and the area of conflict in which they had to defend was on a truly grander scale. On the southern flank of the Eastern Front the Germans lost Rumania and Bulgaria, which consequently left a huge gap through which the Red Army could pour through, heading towards Hungary. The position of Army Group Centre did not fare much better either. The 3rd Panzer Army and the 4th Army, holding a salient in the north, were being steadily ground down by overwhelming Soviet superiority. To the southwest in Poland, along the Narew River, was the 2nd Army. Dwindling forces along the river could not hold for any appreciable time. To make matters worse a number of supporting tanks had simply run out of fuel and had to be abandoned. Dangerously understrength, these forces were supposed to defend the front against over two million Russian soldiers.

But still there was no respite. On 13 January 1945, the Red Army finally opened-up a massive offensive with the 4th Panzer Army taking the full brunt of an artillery barrage followed by an armoured attack by the 1st Byelorrussian Front. It had total numerical superiority over the Germans with 7 to 1 in armour alone. The vast tide of the Red Army soon swallowed up the battlefield and by the end of the first day of the new offensive it had torn a huge breach over 35km wide in the Vistula front.

The 4th Panzer Army had almost ceased to exist. Determinedly though the survivors held out in small groups of grenadiers supported by Panzers, until they too were annihilated or forced to fall back.

One month later the German forces in the East had been driven back to the River Oder, the last bastion of defence before Berlin. Along 240km of the defensive front the remaining Panzer divisions had no more than 70 tanks strung out along the front lines and were almost totally unprotected. A report noted that each division had to hold a frontage of approximately 36km. For every kilometre of front some remaining regiments had one artillery piece, one heavy machine gun, two light machine guns and about 150 men. On every two and a half kilometres of front they had, in addition, one anti-tank gun. On every four kilometres they had one Panzer, and on every six kilometres one battalion. They were confronted by an enemy force made up of three tank armies consisting of thousands of tanks.

Within two months these tank armies would be bearing down towards the outskirts of Berlin. The ragbag force of what was left of the German Army fought out in desperation as the Soviet thrust carved its way across the Oder, capturing the town of Kustrin, and heading towards the Nazi capital. Even during the battle of Berlin the commander of the 503.heavy tank battalion was able to report on 26 April, that he still had six tanks ready for active service in the defence of the routes leading into Berlin.

Both on the Eastern and Western Fronts during the last weeks of the war most of the remaining Panzer divisions continued to fight as a unit until the last days of the war when they destroyed their equipment and surrendered to the enemy. Among the last Panzer divisions of the war formed, in name only, was Panzer-Division 'Clausewitz' which was formed with two battalions of two tank companies each with a total of 56 tanks and assault guns. Although it saw extensive action, its success was limited and localised and did nothing to avert enemy operations.

At the time of surrender, the combined strength of the entire *Panzerwaffe* was 2,023 tanks, 738 assault guns and 159 Flakpanzers. Surprisingly this was the same strength that was used to attack Russia in 1941. But the size of German Army in 1945 was not the same; it was far too inadequate in strength for any type of task. Although the war had ended, the Panzer divisions still existed, but not as the offensive weapon they were in the early Blitzkrieg years.

An interesting photograph taken in 1944 showing a long column of StuG.III. Ausf.G`s on specially adapted railway flatcars, destined for the frontlines in Russia. Note the lashed down tarpaulins on the vehicles. These were meant to protect sensitive parts of the assault guns from dirt, dust and moisture.

Field-Marshal Walter Model inspects a StuG crew during winter operations in Army Group North in early February 1944. Model was nicknamed the Führer`s `fireman` for his trouble shooting tactics. He was probably the most effective German General on the Eastern Front during the reverses in Russia, and managed to stabilize the northern sector of the front in February 1944.

A halftrack with a full compliment of crew tows a PaK 40 anti-tank gun along a muddy road in Russia in March 1944. The soldiers are wearing the reversible grey/white two-piece winter suit. When the men wore the garments white side out they quickly became discoloured with dirt and grime, and soon lost their effectiveness as a camouflage piece of clothing.

Panzer crewmen belonging to an unidentified Panzer regiment pose for the camera in early June 1944. Behind them is a column of Pz.Kpfw.IV`s. Within three weeks of this photograph being taken the Red Army would unleash operation `Bagration` which was launched against Army Group Centre. Almost 900 Panzers were destroyed as a result.

A StuG.III Ausf.G, one of many armoured vehicles scraped together, prepares to journey east in the summer of 1944. This was in a drastic attempt to help the war effort by propping-up the disintegrating German front lines.

A Late variant Pz.Kpfw.IV halts on a road on the border with Yugoslavia in the summer of 1944. This vehicle is just one of many that was hastily sent from Germany to the Bulgarian Army on direct orders from Hitler.

In western Russia a Pz.Kpfw.IV Ausf.H with intact Schürzen moves along a dirt track. Its three digit tactical number '134' is painted in red on the side of the turret. Although difficult to see, the vehicle is painted with a camouflage scheme of light green spots over the dark sand base.

A Pz.Kpfw.IV moves along a muddy road at the edge of a forest during operations in Yugoslavia in 1944. The vehicle has clearly received an application of winter white wash paint. The soldiers supporting the Panzers drive are from the Bulgarian Army. They are all wearing German standard issue uniforms.

A Pz.Kpfw.IV during operations in the Balkans in 1944. During this period a substantial amount of German armour was sent to the area in an attempt to defend from advancing Red Army forces and to help the Germans pacify Marshal Tito's communist guerrillas that now numbered well over 100,000 men.

Bulgarian soldiers supported by a StuG.III. Ausf.G move along a mountain road during anti-guerrilla operations in the Balkans. When the Bulgarian government finally declared war against Germany in September 1944, a number of Bulgarian units were still used in the Balkans in preparation for the Soviet invasion. But no Bulgarian forces were ever used against the Red Army.

A column of Bulgarian Pz.Kpfw.IV`s halt inside a village somewhere in the Balkans in 1944. The Pz.Kpfw.IV was known by the Bulgarians as the Maybach T-IV. Altogether 46 units of them were obtained from the Germans. However, when the Red Army finally marched into Bulgaria in late October 1944, the 150,000-strong Bulgarian army went over to its sides including the bulk of the German armour.

The Bulgarian Army show off some of their new Pz.Kpfw.IV`s, courtesy of the *Panzerwaffe*. These vehicles would be used in the Balkans against Yugoslavian or Greek guerrilla units, which were constantly hampering the German war effort.

Bulgarian forces on parade in 1944 with Pz.Kpfw.IV`s and Renault R-35`s, which were basically used as ammunition carriers. The Germans had happily sent armour to the Bulgarians who they believed to be the most reliable of the Balkan allies because of their hatred of the Greeks and their fear of the Turks.

A Marder.III is stationary in a field with two of the crewmembers relaxing. The third crewmember is examining one of the shells. The vehicle's fighting compartment can be seen protected by a canvas hood. The barrel's muzzle brake has a protective covering as well. This vehicle was a very effective weapon and provided the Panzer divisions, especially during the later period of the war, with a good mobile anti-tank capability.

An interesting photograph showing Panzergrenadiers being trained in Poland during the early summer of 1944. Sd.Kfz.251 halftracks can be seen moving across the training ground, whilst grenadiers armed with MG 34 machine guns have improvised by digging slit trenches. Panzergrenadiers were the German motorized infantry and, because they were required so urgently for battle, training was often limited.

A halftrack towing a Pak anti-tank gun passes burning buildings in Poland. By August 1944 the Red Army had arrived at the banks of the River Vistula. The 4th Panzer Army had been given the task to hold the river at all costs. Although under pressure from large Russian tank forces, the German Panzer defence was organized in depth and held firm, but only temporarily.

Supported by a Pz.Kpfw.IV, Panzergrenadiers move through a Polish town that has evidently experienced some heavy fighting. The Panzergrenadiers were always used in the thick of battle and provided the advancing armour with valuable support.

A halftrack towing a Pak 40 anti-tank gun during operations in Hungary in December 1944. The Pak crew are wearing their winter reversible garments. For local defence one soldier is armed with an MG 42 machine gun, which can just be seen perched on the canvas roof of the vehicle.

An Sd.Kfz.250 and a StuG.III Ausf.G are parked with full winter white wash camouflage in Hungary in late 1944. These vehicles belong to an unidentified Panzer regiment of the 23.Panzer-Division and are resting following heavy clashes with Soviet forces.

Tiger tank crewman load shells through the loader's roof hatch during a pause in fighting in Poland. Of the total ammunition load of 92 rounds, a well-stocked crew would have half armour piercing shells and half high explosive shells. Occasionally, when available, a few rounds of high velocity sub-calibre, tungsten core shells were used by the crews, which were carried specifically against heavy Russian armour.

The commander of a Nashorn tank destroyer poses for the camera next to his potent 8.8cm Pak 43 duel anti-tank/anti-aircraft gun. The Nashorn was introduced in time for the battle of the Kursk and soon proved to be a highly effective tank killer until it was replaced in late 1944 by the Jagdpanzer IV and Jagdpanther.

In Poland a group of troops pose for the camera in front of an Sd.Kfz.7 prime mover in the late winter of 1944. The Panzer divisions in Poland were now faced with a more dangerous and worsening prospect than ever before. Armoured strength had gone far beyond the danger point. Out of a total production of 2,299 tanks and assault guns manufactured during this period, only 921 of them reached the Eastern Front.

A column of German PoWs escorted by Russian troops pass a destroyed Jagdpanzer IV/70 tank destroyer in Hungary in January 1945. The Jagdpanzer was an effective tank destroyer, but by the time it left the manufacturers its unique defensive attributes mattered little anymore.

A StuG.III Ausf.G belonging to an unidentified assault gun battery advances along a muddy track on the German/Polish border in January 1945. On 20 January advanced elements of the Red Army finally arrived on German soil.

The crew of a command Tiger.I scour the terrain ahead trying to deduce the location of the advancing enemy. Although the Tiger was still regarded as a deadly tank, the Allies had developed weapons to counter the Tiger's impact on the battlefield. The British introduced the Sherman Firefly, which was armed with a 17-pounder super-velocity gun. It was more deadly than the Tiger's 8.8cm gun. The tank-busting Typhoon fighter also carried armour-piercing rockets, which were more than a match for the Tiger's armour. The Russians too had developed 100mm and 152mm guns that could destroy the Tiger. By the end of the war, other tanks had been developed that outclassed the Tiger – the Joseph Stalin II and the American M26 Pershing was among them.

Panzergrenadiers move forward towards the River Oder supported by a StuG.III. During the last year of the war the number of Panzergrenadier divisions continued to grow. With the mounting losses of men and armour the Panzergrenadiers displayed outstanding ability and endurance in the face of overwhelming odds.

The crew of a StuG.III Ausf.G converse with their commander before commencing further battlefield duties against allied forces in western Germany in March 1945. Note the German M42 steel helmets attached to the assault gun for additional armoured protection.

Panzergrenadiers dismount from an early Panther Ausf.G during the last months of the war in Germany. The Panzergrenadier standing at the front of the *Panther* is holding an MG42 machine gun. By this period of the war, Panzergrenadiers were not so much supporting the tanks as being supported by them.

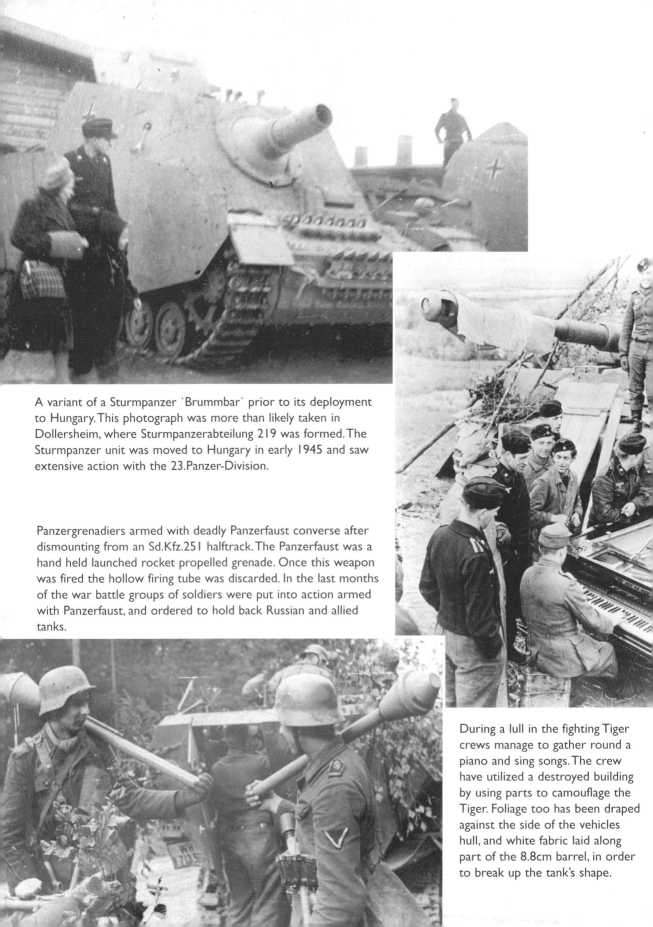

A variant of a Sturmpanzer `Brummbar` prior to its deployment to Hungary. This photograph was more than likely taken in Dollersheim, where Sturmpanzerabteilung 219 was formed. The Sturmpanzer unit was moved to Hungary in early 1945 and saw extensive action with the 23.Panzer-Division.

Panzergrenadiers armed with deadly Panzerfaust converse after dismounting from an Sd.Kfz.251 halftrack. The Panzerfaust was a hand held launched rocket propelled grenade. Once this weapon was fired the hollow firing tube was discarded. In the last months of the war battle groups of soldiers were put into action armed with Panzerfaust, and ordered to hold back Russian and allied tanks.

During a lull in the fighting Tiger crews manage to gather round a piano and sing songs. The crew have utilized a destroyed building by using parts to camouflage the Tiger. Foliage too has been draped against the side of the vehicles hull, and white fabric laid along part of the 8.8cm barrel, in order to break up the tank's shape.

A Sturmpanzer `Brummbar` has run out of fuel and sits on a road in a captured town somewhere in the Ruhr pocket. American soldiers can be seen marching past. This vehicle was part of Sturmpanzerabteilung 217, which had withdrawn through Holland and fought in the defence of Aachen and the Ruhr Pocket.

A very rare photograph showing a brand new Panzerjäger Tiger (P) Elefant Tank Destroyer being prepared to be transported through Germany on board a railway flatcar. The Elefant was one of the first German vehicles to carry the long-barrelled Pak 43/2 L/71 8.8cm flak gun.

A Pz.Kpfw.IV kicks up a cloud of dust as it travels along a road towards the front lines in the summer of 1944. Even during the last year of the war the Pz.Kpfw.IV continued to play a dominant role in the Panzer divisions.

One of the quickest methods of transporting armour from one front to another was by rail. Here a Panzerjäger Tiger and Elefant tank destroyer in winter whitewash has been chocked and secured ready for its journey by rail. Due to their sheer size and weight, no more than six of these Elefant tank destroyers were permitted to be loaded on one train. These were interspersed with two flatcars to avoid overloading of the trains, and also to prevent overloading of the bridges.

An Elefant tank destroyer stationary on a road with its crew during operations in the later stages of the war. This vehicle saw its debut at Kursk in July 1943 and was able to defeat all types of Soviet tanks, but they lacked cross-country mobility and were prone to breakdowns. Also, with no secondary armament they were vulnerable to infantry armed with magnetic mines and charges.

A captured *Jagdtiger* on a Gotha 80 tonne trailer being prepared to be taken to England for inspection. Although the firepower of *Jagdtiger* was lethal, its mobility was restricted mainly due to fuel shortages and mechanical breakdowns. They were also very slow moving and a relatively easy target to allied fighter-bombers.

A Pz.Kpfw.IV advances along a road. Until the very end of the war the Pz.Kpfw.IV remained the most popular Panzer in the Panzer divisions and played a significant role, despite the battlefield inferiority. Even during the battle of Berlin in April 1945, the Pz.Kpfw.IV fought tenaciously until they were either captured or destroyed.

A Hummel advances across a devastated wasteland somewhere in eastern Germany in March 1945. The surrounding buildings have been destroyed by allied bombing attacks. The vehicle is not embroiled in combat as one of the crewmembers can be seen casually sitting on the 15cm barrel.

A Panzergrenadier in early April 1945 is about to scour the local terrain with his Zeiss binoculars, trying to locate the enemy's position. The muzzle break of a StuG.III Ausf.G can be seen poised for action.

A completely destroyed Pz.Kpfw.IV stands next to a charred tree. The Panzer has obviously had a violent explosion on board with its turret virtually blown off. Amazingly the vehicle's tracks are still intact. All the crew would have undoubtedly been killed instantly as a result of the direct hit.

A British soldier examines a knocked out Tiger tank in April 1945. The Tiger has clearly been hit at the side, as twisted skirting is evident from the shells' impact. The loss of the tank track obviously immobilized the vehicle, prompting the crew to bail out. It is unknown whether the crew cannibalised the Tiger first and removed the MG 34 machine gun.

153

Civilians stand next to an abandoned *Jagdpanzer Hetzer* 38 (t). The vehicle has more than likely run out of fuel and the crew have hastily abandoned it as a result. By 1945 there not many *Hezter`s* left in service fighting alongside the Panzer divisions. Between February and April 1945, as Germany lurched towards defeat, there were even fewer *Hezter`s* reaching the front line combat units.

A StuG.III Ausf.G has been knocked out during the battle of Berlin. This photograph was taken just a few days after the Soviet capture of the Reich capital. Because the StuG had no traversing turret it was not very adaptable in urbanized combat and was easy prey to Soviet anti-tank gunners. However, by the end of the war there were some 738-assault guns still in service alongside the once vaunted Panzer divisions.

Panzer Division
Glossary

1. Panzer-Division
Formed October 1935 at Weimer.

Units:
Panzer Regiment 1
Panzer Artillery Regiment 73
Panzergrenadier Regiment 1, 113
Panzer Aufkl Abt (Reconnaissance Section) 1.

Theatres of Operation:
Poland 1939
Belgium and France 1940
Northern and Central Groups Russia June
1941-February 1943
Balkans and Greece 1943
Ukraine November-December 1943
Hungary and Austria June 1944-May 1945

2. Panzer-Division
Formed October 1935 at Wurzburg

Units:
Panzergrenadier Regiment 2, 304
Panzer Regiment 3
Panzer Artillery Regiment 74
Panzer Aufkl Abt (Reconnaissance) 2

Theatres of Operation:
Poland 1939
France 1940
Balkans and Greece 1941
Army Group Centre (Smolensk, Orel, Kiev)
1942-43
France and Germany 1944-45

3. Panzer-Division
Formed October 1935 at Berlin

Units:
Panzergrenadier Regiments 3, 394
Panzer Regiment 6
Panzer Artillery Regiment 75
Panzer Aufkl Abt 3

Theatres of Operation:
Poland 1939

France 1940
Central Russia 1941-42
Southern Russia – Kharkov and Dnepr Bend 1943
Ukraine and Poland 1944
Hungary and Austria 1944-45

4. Panzer-Division
Formed November 1938 at Wurzburg

Units:
Panzergrenadier Regiment 12, 33
Panzer Regiment 35
Panzer Artillery Regiment 103
Panzer Aufkl Abt 4

Theatres of Operation:
Poland 1939
France 1940
Central Russia-Caucasus 1942, Kursk 1943
   and Latvia 1944
Germany 1945

5.Panzer-Division
Formed at Oppeln in November 1939

Units:
Panzergrenadier Regiments 13, 14
Panzer Regiment 31
Panzer Artillery Regiment 116
Panzer Aufkl Abt 5

Theatres of Operation:
France 1941
Yugoslavia and Greece 1941
Central Russia – Kursk, Dnepr, Latvia, and
Kurland 1941-44
East Prussia 1944-45

6. Panzer-Division
Formed at Wuppertal in October 1939

Units:
Panzergrenadier Regiment 4, 114
Panzer Regiment 11
Panzer Artillery Regiment 76
Panzer Aufkl Abt 6

Theatres of Operation:
France 1944
Russia 1941-44
Hungary and Austria 1944-45

7. Panzer-Division
Formed at Weimar in October 1939

Units:
Panzergrenadier Regiments 6, 7
Panzer Regiment 25
Panzer Artillery Regiment 78
Panzer Aufkl Abt 7

Theatres of Operation:
France 1940
Central Russia 1941
Refit in France 1942
Southern Russia 1942
Kharkov 1942
Baltic Coast and Prussia 1944-45

8. Panzer-Division
Formed at Berlin in October 1938

Units:
Panzergrenadier Regiments 8, 28
Panzer Regiment 10
Panzer Artillery Regiment 80
Panzer Aufkl Abt 8

Theatres of Operation:
Holland and France 1940
Balkans 1941
Southern Russia 1941
Central Russia 1942
Kursk 1943
France 1944
Ardennes Offensive 1944-45

10.Panzer-Division
Formed in April 1939 at Stuttgart

Units:
Panzergrenadier Regiments 69, 86
Panzer Regiment 7
Panzer Artillery Regiment 90
Panzer Aufkl Abt 10

Theatres of Operation:
Poland 1939
France 1940
France 1942
Tunisia 1943 (Division Destroyed)

11.Panzer-Division
Formed August 1940 at Breslau

Units:
Panzergrenadier Regiments 110, 111
Panzer Regiment 15
Panzer Artillery Regiment 119
Panzer Aufkl Abt 11

Theatres of Operation:
Balkans 1941
Russia 1941-44 (Orel, Belgorod, Krivoi Rog
    and Korsun)
Northern France 1944

12.Panzer-Division
Formed in October 1940

Units:
Panzergrenadier Regiments 5, 25
Panzer Regiment 29
Panzer Artillery Regiment 2
Panzer Aufkl Abt 12

Theatres of Operation:
Russia Army Group Centre 1941-44
Russia 1941 Minsk and Smolensk
Leningrad 1942
Orel and Middle Dnepr 1943
Kurland 1945 (Captured By the Red Army)

13.Panzer-Division
Formed in October 1940

Units:
Panzergrenadier Regiments 66, 93
Panzer Regiment 4
Panzer Artillery Regiment 13
Panzer Aufkl Abt 13

Theatre of Operations:
Rumania 1941
Russia 1941-44
Kiev 1942
Caucasus and the Kuban 1943-44
Krivoi Rog 1944
Germany 1944
Hungary 1944-45

14.Panzer-Division
Formed in August 1940

Units:
Panzergrenadier Regiments 103, 108
Panzer Regiment 36

Panzer Artillery Regiment 4
Panzer Aufkl Abt 14

Theatres of Operation:
Yugoslavia 1941
Germany 1941
Hungary 1941
Yugoslavia 1941
Southern Russia 1941
December 1942 (Completely Decimated at
　Stalingrad)

15.Panzer-Division
Formed in August 1940

Units:
Panzergrenadier Regiments 104, 115
Panzer Regiment 8
Panzer Artillery Regiment 33
Panzer Aufkl Abt 15

Theatres of Operation:
North Africa 1941-43
(Surrendered In Tunisia in 1943)

16.Panzer-Division
Formed in August 1940

Units:
Panzergrenadier Regiments 64, 79
Panzer Regiment 2
Panzer Artillery Regiment 16
Panzer Aufkl Abt 16

Theatres of Operation:
Southern Russia 1941
December 1942 (Completely Decimated at
　Stalingrad)
Reformed In France 1943
Italy 1943
Russia- Kiev 1943-45

17.Panzer-Division
Formed in October 1940

Units:
Panzergrenadier Regiments 40, 63
Panzer Regiment 39
Panzer Artillery Regiment 27
Panzer Aufkl Abt 17

Theatres of Operation:
Russia (Central and Southern Sectors)
　1941-45

18.Panzer-Division
Formed in October 1940

Major Units:
Panzergrenadier Regiments 52, 101
Panzer Regiment 18
Panzer Artillery Regiment 88
Panzer Aufkl Abt 8

Theatres of Operation:
Russia (Central and Southern Sectors) 1941-43

19.Panzer-Division
Formed in October 1940

Major Units:
Panzergrenadier Regiments 73, 74
Panzer Regiment 27
Panzer Artillery Regiment 19
Panzer Aufkl Abt 19

Theatres of Operation:
1941-44 (Russian Central and Southern Sectors)

20.Panzer-Division
Formed in October 1940

Major Units:
Panzergrenadier Regiments 59, 112
Panzer Regiment 21
Panzer Artillery Regiment 92
Panzer Aufkl Abt 20

Theatres of Operations:
Russia 1941-44
Moscow 1941
Orel 1943
Rumania 1944
East Prussia 1944
Hungary 1944

21.Panzer-Division
Formed in the field during February 1941

Units:
Panzergrenadier Regiments 125, 192
Panzer Regiment 22
Panzer Artillery Regiment 155
Panzer Aufkl Abt 21

Theatres of Operations:
North Africa 1941-43
Northern France 1944
Eastern Front 1945

22.Panzer-Division
Formed in October 1941 in France

Units:
Panzergrenadier Regiments 129, 140
Panzer Regiment 204
Panzer Artillery Regiment 140
Panzer Aufkl Abt 140

Theatres of Operations:
Russia Central Front 1942 (Almost
Decimated At Stalingrad)

23.Panzer-Division
Formed in October 1941 in France

Units:
Panzergrenadier Regiments 126, 128
Panzer Regiment 23
Panzer Artillery Regiment 128
Panzer Aufkl Abt 23

Theatres of Operation:
Russia 1942 – 1944
Kharkov 1943
Stalingrad 1943
Caucasus 1943
Dnepr Bend 1944
Poland 1944 (Refit)
Hungary 1944

24.Panzer-Division
Formed in February 1942

Units:
Panzergrenadier Regiments 21, 26
Panzer Regiment 24
Panzer Artillery Regiment 89
Panzer Aufkl Abt 24

Theatres of Operation:
Russian 1942
Stalingrad 1942 (Decimated At Stalingrad)
Northern France 1943 (Reformed)
Russia 1943
Kiev and Dnepr bend 1943
Poland 1944
Hungary 1944
Slovakia 1944
Germany 1945

25.Panzer-Division
Formed in February 1942 from units in Norway

Units:
Panzergrenadier Regiments 146, 147

Panzer Regiment 9
Panzer Artillery Regiment 91
Panzer Aufkl Abt 25

Theatres of Operation:
Russia Southern sector 1943
Kiev 1943
Denmark 1944 (Refit)
Poland 1944
Germany 1945

26.Panzer-Division
Formed in Brittany during October 1942

Units:
Panzergrenadier Regiments 9, 67
Panzer Regiment 26
Panzer Artillery Regiment 93
Panzer Aufkl Abt 26

Theatres of Operation:
Italy 1943-44

27.Panzer-Division
Formed in France 1942

(Disbanded Early Due Heavy Casualties in
early 1943)

116.Panzer-Division
Formed in France in 1944

Units:
Panzergrenadier Regiments 60, 156
Panzer Regiment 16
Panzer Artillery Regiment 146
Panzer Aufkl Abt 116

Theatres of Operations:
France 1944
Ardennes 1944
Kleve 1945

The Panzer-Lehr-Division
Formed in France in 1944

Units:
Panzergrenadier Regiments 901, 902
Panzer Regiment 103
Panzer Artillery Regiment 130
Panzer Aufkl Abt 130

Theatres of Operation:
France 1944
Ardennes 1944
Holland 1944
Germany 1944

Divisional Insignia

1st Panzer	7th Panzer	13th Panzer	19th Panzer
2nd Panzer	8th Panzer	14th Panzer	20th Panzer
3rd Panzer	9th Panzer	15th Panzer	21st Panzer
4th Panzer	10th Panzer	16th Panzer	22nd Panzer
5th Panzer	11th Panzer	17th Panzer	23rd Panzer
6th Panzer	12th Panzer	18th Panzer	24th Panzer

Divisional Insignia

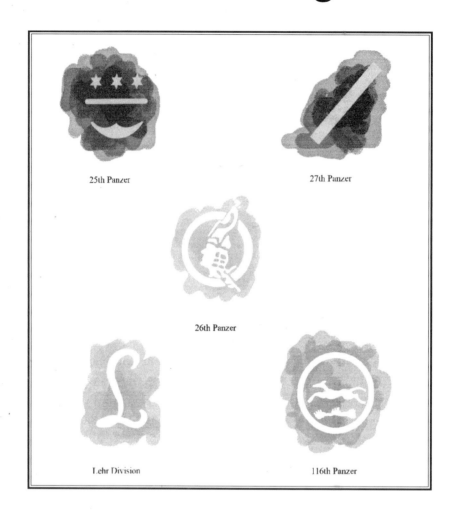

25th Panzer

27th Panzer

26th Panzer

Lehr Division

116th Panzer